Writer's Triangle
A Literature-Based Writing Program

Carla Heymsfeld and Joan Lewis

Fearon Teacher Aids
Belmont, California

Simon & Schuster Supplementary Education Group

Designed by: Rose Sheifer
Illustrations by: Duane Bibby

ISBN 0-8224-7496-4

Printed in the United States of America

1.98765432

Contents

Introduction

▲
The Purpose

The major goals are to expose students in grades 5-8 to fine literature and to train them to examine and understand writing techniques used by successful authors. Students then learn to apply this knowledge to improve and edit their own writing. They have an opportunity to experience fine literature in three ways: reading books themselves, listening to books read aloud by their teacher, and seeing filmstrips of books.

Students in grades 5-8 find these films and read-alouds stimulating and motivating. Strong readers in the sixth grade are usually able to handle even the more difficult books, and older, weaker readers generally find most of the simply written stories sophisticated enough to hold their interest. Teachers should use the summary and comments on the introductory page for each book to help them make decisions about which titles are most appropriate for their classes.

Each of the three experiences is followed by carefully planned discussions and by writing assignments that are direct outgrowths of the discussions. For example, if one of the discussion questions is about how an author sets a mood of mystery, the ensuing writing assignment might be to create an opening paragraph for a mystery story.

▲
The Format

In each literary experience, children are guided through a carefully structured procedure that emphasizes critical thinking skills.

1. The **Prereading Focus** is a motivator that bridges students' present knowledge and the ideas they will encounter in the book and helps students look for the author's techniques and ideas.

2. Students **read** a book, **watch** a filmstrip, or **listen** to a book read aloud.

3. A brief **factual test** for books read independently helps the teacher evaluate students' readiness to participate in a meaningful discussion.

4. Students apply to their **own writing** some aspect of content or structure of the novel.

5. Students **evaluate and revise** their writing, armed with suggestions from a group conference. The emphasis is on the writing skill highlighted by the lesson.

The filmstrips and read-alouds can be used at any point in the program. Some teachers may wish to begin Writer's Triangle by having the shared experience of a filmstrip or a read-aloud. Others may prefer to begin with a book, interspersing the films and read-alouds throughout the remainder of the program to provide variety. In classes where the students' reading ability is low, teachers can lean heavily on the filmstrips, read-alouds, and books that have accompanying tapes. In this way it is possible to provide instruction in literary analysis and writing to students who would otherwise be closed out of such an experience.

The Philosophy

Why is integration of the areas of language arts so important?

▼ Each language arts area supports the others, and the skills to handle one are analogous to the skills needed to handle the other effectively.

▼ Integration of reading, writing, and listening avoids overlap. In a crowded curriculum it is the most efficient way to teach.

▼ Discussion helps students appreciate varied interpretations as they focus their own understanding of literature. In turn, students process these insights internally as they incorporate them in their own writing.

Why supplement a basal program with outstanding children's literature?

▼ A novel's complex narrative structure induces deeper, more sophisticated understandings than short basal selections.

▼ The best books involve emotional as well as cognitive experience, thus engaging both the right and left hemispheres of the brain. This opens the way for more complex learning.

▼ Novels about other boys and girls help students to learn about themselves and to explore values and choices safely.

▼ Novels stimulate our imaginations and make the past and the future come alive, allowing us to know people who are different from ourselves.

How does hearing and reading literature improve writing?

▼ Literature provides a model. Students need to see how others use language, construct plots, create characters, invent settings, and develop interesting dialogue.

▼ By examining the choices and strategies used by an excellent writer, students can put themselves in a writer's shoes and learn to make similar choices and use similar strategies in their own writing.

How does writing improve the ability to read and understand literature?

▼ Organizing their own writing forces students to focus on skills, such as main idea, sequence, or cause and effect, that are traditionally taught in reading programs.

▼ Creating their own structures, characters, and settings helps students look for and appreciate them in literature.

Why include read-aloud books and filmstrips of books?

▼ A multidimensional approach accommodates students' varied learning styles. All children benefit from exposure to many forms of representation, and children who learn best from concrete experience benefit from the visual and auditory stimulation of a filmstrip. Moreover, compression of a novel into a filmstrip allows students to grasp the author's vision quickly.

▼ Students of all abilities enjoy these activities. A pleasurable experience creates interest in good literature, motivating them to read.

▼ A teacher who reads a book aloud has an opportunity to model involvement and pleasure in reading and is able to share the experience with students.

The Program

SCHEDULE

Choose as many books as class time and funds permit. One book sequence takes about a month to complete. You must also consider other components of your reading program. If Writer's Triangle is an addition to a complete basal program, you will be able to handle fewer novels than if you are using novels exclusively.

When you are starting students, plan to allow about 15 minutes for them to get their books, participate in the prereading discussion with their group, understand the Prereading Focus guidelines, and fill in their target due dates.

Although books can be read at home, it is highly motivating to allow students class time to do their reading. Research shows that independent silent reading in school as well as at home has a beneficial effect on student reading skills.

Students need 15 minutes for the Fact Check Test and an hour for the discussion of the novel. It is wise to allow two days between the Fact Check Test and the discussion so that students whose test scores indicate that they are not yet ready to participate fully in the discussion can use this time to finish or reread the book.

During this discussion period, allow students at least 40 minutes to discuss their book. Leave 20 minutes to explain the writing assignment and give students a chance to begin their writing. Combining these two activities in one session helps students see the connections between reading and writing and makes their writing efforts more productive.

Additional in-class writing time is another significant factor toward good participation in Writer's Triangle. It tells students that the teacher values their writing and that the program is an integral part of the curriculum.

Finally, schedule a second hour for writing conferences, with about ten students in each group. Every student needs time to share writing, learn what peers enjoy, and hear suggestions for improvement.

SUGGESTED SCHEDULE FOR ONE SEQUENCE

Activity	Day	Class Time
Get books	Day 1	10 minutes
Fact Check Test	Day 14	15 minutes
Discussion	Day 16	1 hour
First draft	Day 23	1 hour
Final draft	Day 30	——

INTRODUCING THE PROGRAM

Explain the goals of Writer's Triangle and the various components of the program to your class. Emphasize that students get to make some choices. They will select the books they'll read from *your* Writer's

Triangle list. As you introduce the novels to your class, give them time to look over the annotations. Make sure you tell them which books have lots of action, which ones emphasize character development, and which ones include intriguing descriptive writing, so that they can make good decisions about what they will enjoy reading. They also need to know which books are the most difficult and which ones are a little easier.

STUDENTS PRIORITIZE READING LISTS

Give each student a priority list that includes all the books you will be making available to them (see Priority List, p. 17). Ask your class to put the books they wish to read in order of priority. If you're working with ten novels during the year, students should put *1* by the book they wish to read more than any other and *10* by the one they wish to read less than any other.

Explain to your class that you will try to give them their top choices, although you may have to ask them to read one that is not at the top of their list. This is because, after every student has read several books, their remaining choices may be scattered and not fall neatly into three (or whatever number of reading groups you're working with) groups. This grouping problem can be solved in one of three ways: (1) by bringing in another adult leader and forming an extra group, (2) by rescheduling so that you can handle the group yourself, or (3) by asking students to read a book that is not one of their top choices. The simplest solution is the last one, but it should be used with caution.

EVALUATION SYSTEM

Consider how to evaluate your student's work. Since enthusiastic, on-time participation is the key to success, we have found the following guidelines help students focus their efforts and meet target dates.

▼ The Fact Check Test is graded traditionally, allowing ten points for each question.

▼ Give those students who are effective discussion group members 100 percent for the discussion. Students who do not participate because they haven't read the book earn a 0. Use judgment in grading infrequent contributors whose Fact Check Test indicates they've read the book. Remember, the purpose of these ratings is to encourage students to read, reflect, and enjoy sharing their ideas.

▼ All students who hand in a reasonable first draft effort on time deserve 100 percent for their first draft. Penalize late contributors by lowering their evaluation one letter grade for every day late.

▼ Students who show effort at improving style and content on their final draft deserve a 100 percent for it. Students who turn in late final papers are penalized a grade per day, and students whose final papers reflect little recognition of conference suggestions or effort at improvement deserve an appropriately lower grade.

▼ Essentially, students who turn work in on time and make an effort to improve do well.

Since on-time participation is critical to the success of Writer's Triangle, emphasize to your students that effort and completing assignments by the target dates are the keys to an A. Students gain confidence and enthusiasm when they realize they have a good chance at a top grade even if they are not usually "top" readers. Make a transparency of the introductory example chart in order to show students the grades of those who procrastinate (see Grading, p. 18). On this example, points are lowered by 25 percent for late papers so that students can more easily see the impact of effort and on-time participation. Explain that *learning to manage how long it takes to read a novel and complete a writing assignment is a major benefit of Writer's Triangle.* Give students ample time to ask questions and voice concerns so that you can demonstrate a warm, open manner that will set the stage for productive discussion and conferences.

READING GROUPS

Using the priority lists and your knowledge of reading levels and leadership skills among your students, select a well-balanced group of about six to ten students to read each book. Try to give students their top priority as soon as possible. If you are planning to run more than one group at a time, begin by forming one workable group. Then compose additional well-balanced groups for one or two other books. Composing groups is easier if you make separate stacks of priority lists for each title under consideration. An individual student's list can easily be moved from pile to pile until you've achieved your goal of groups that will work well together. At this point you may need to ask a student if he or she would read a book that was not a top priority. Most students are quite willing to compromise. This is the time to suggest an easier book for a student who has selected one far above his or her capabilities. After you decide which book a student will read, put a check next to its corresponding number on the priority list so that you can keep track of who has read what.

We have indicated which novels in Writer's Triangle are available on tape. If you have students who would benefit from listening to a tape, establish an in-class listening center for them, either in your room or in the school library. Explain that the tape will help them more fully appreciate the story, but it is incomplete and cannot take the place of reading the book. All students need to be reminded that they may have to read some parts of their book more than once, especially if they're chosen a difficult novel. The increased understanding that comes with rereading brings satisfaction and success.

KEEPING TRACK

Type your students' names on the management chart (see Management Chart, p. 19). Write an abbreviation of the titles your class will read above the columns on the top right section of the chart. Duplicate one copy of the chart for each book sequence during the year, and keep the extras in reserve. Make a check in the appropriate column for the book each student will read during the sequence. Highlighting each book column helps separate groups if your class is reading several books during a sequence. If other teachers, such as the reading specialist or librarian, are also supervising groups, write their names at the top of their novel columns and duplicate copies of the management chart for them to use.

Fill in the target dates for all assignments on the schedule section at the bottom of the chart. Duplicate this schedule on construction paper and post it in your classroom so that students can fill in due dates on their Prereading Focus sheets. Having a target date chart posted in your classroom helps keep everyone on track.

As students complete assignments, record their grades on your chart. If other teachers are supervising groups, they record and average the grades on their charts and give them to you when assignments are completed.

If you have a computer with a spreadsheet program, you can design a spreadsheet management system that will quickly average your grades. Make sure it's set up with novel columns on the right side of the page so that you can check off titles and use just one piece of paper to manage each Writer's Triangle sequence.

FILMSTRIPS AND READ-ALOUDS

Management of the filmstrip and read-aloud components are similar to management of the novel component. When using a filmstrip, schedule the second part of a two-part film anytime within a week of the first viewing. The first writing draft should be due a week later. Ask your librarian to show the filmstrip and take part of the class for discussion and conferences. Students will benefit from a lower pupil-per-teacher ratio, and it is an excellent way to integrate library and classroom curricula.

The read-alouds have been paced for about 20 minutes of reading time per session. Try to read daily to maintain continuity and interest. Allow time for discussion at the end of each reading session.

STUDENTS' EVALUATIONS

1. *Discussion Self-evaluation.* Successful discussion sessions occur when students participate fully, demonstrating that they have achieved target goals and mastered procedures. Self-evaluation of their performance helps them focus more clearly on behaviors that ensure success. Students and teachers can look at the evaluation forms and quickly spot areas that need improvement for certain individuals or for the entire group (see Student Discussion Self-evaluation, p. 21).

2. *End-of-Year Evaluation.* Students appreciate classroom situations in which their opinions are valued. Yearly assessment of Writer's Triangle by both students and teachers will produce a program that works best for your particular situation (see End-of-Year Evaluation, p. 22).

Successful Discussions

Novel discussion groups are significantly influenced by the atmosphere within the classroom before the students meet to discuss the book. It is most important that the *teacher* create an open atmosphere of mutual respect and give students many opportunities to practice cooperative behavior.

Clear goals and procedures for effective group membership must be established and taught by the teacher. Students need to know that they must be prepared to discuss the novel, use examples from the book to support their ideas, and stay on the topic. With some classes it may also be necessary to set goals related to public speaking, such as talking clearly and loudly enough to be heard and maintaining eye contact with the group.

Establishing the importance of listening, taking turns, and not interrupting others teaches consideration for the viewpoints of others and helps participants learn to build on areas of agreement. Students also need to understand the value of asking questions when they don't understand the ideas of other participants and when parts of the book seem unclear.

After providing clear goals for the discussion, teachers act as coaches. A good leader avoids dominating the discussion and serves instead as a facilitator by stimulating, assisting, and clarifying. Research shows that one of the best ways to keep students open and thinking is to utilize "wait time." After asking questions, teachers should give students time to collect their thoughts, and they should wait at least three seconds before responding to students' answers.

Another way to keep students open and thinking is to give them opportunities to reflect on their participation in the group. Ending each discussion with an evaluation (see p. 12 and Student Discussion Self-evaluation, p.21) helps them focus more clearly on strategies for success.

Successful Writing Conferences

Writing conferences offer many teaching and sharing opportunities for both students and teachers. Students have a chance to share their writing with an audience. The feedback they get on their own work and the exposure they get to the work of others can make a huge contribution to their development as writers. From the teacher's point of view, writing conferences provide the opportunity to shift attention away from the products students turn in and toward the process by which they create them. Teachers who become involved at this formative stage find that they can have greater impact on student writing. Moreover, writing conferences can be occasions for the kind of informal, personal contact with children that sometimes seems prohibited by traditional classroom hierarchy.

Six to ten students is a good size for a group. This allows every student a turn to read and respond to the writing of group members. To be successful, the writing conference's main purpose should be support and help for the author. The job of the group is not to attack the piece; its job is to help the author see it with fresh vision. The group can show the author what was entertaining, touching, confusing, or incomplete, so the author can revise the piece and better achieve what was originally intended or what is now seen as possible.

Whatever your specific goal for an assignment, if you are going to try to work toward it in a group conference, it is critical for the group to be committed to *careful listening*. People cannot respond fairly if, during the time the author is reading, they are working on their own pieces or daydreaming or talking to a neighbor. An author should be able to expect the undivided attention of the audience.

Once the piece is read, the most helpful way to launch the conference is by responding positively: reacting to the content and style of the piece and telling the author what was good about it. If this is your students' first experience with a conference, they may not know how to help each other by identifying specific strengths. You may have to model the procedure for a while, but the group should catch on soon.

Every piece has strengths, and the more specific we can be about them, the better. It is nice for students to hear that people liked their piece; it is even more useful to hear that they liked the way it began. It is good for students to hear that the audience thought their piece was funny; it is more helpful to hear that the discription of the way the dog walked down the street was funny. Positive feedback about specific strengths is important not only because it massages authors' egos, but also because it helps build a body of information about how to do certain writing tasks successfully.

Since the prime purpose of the conference is to help the author, the author should now have a chance to indicate if there is some area where he or she needs help. If there is, addressing this area should be the major concern of the group.

If the author is not aware of problems, then the members of the group can begin to respond on their own. A good place to begin is with clarity. Is there anything that the audience could not understand, a connection that was unclear, a sentence that was garbled? What did you mean by . . . ? and What were you trying to say when . . . ? are questions that can help show authors where they have not communicated what they intended.

Beginning writers often seem constricted. They write a few terse sentences that only begin to suggest the depth and extent of their ideas. Here is where questions about what else happened, about what characters looked like, what they said, or what they felt like help the author see what additional details would enhance the piece.

Sometimes there doesn't seem to be a clear main idea in a student's work. Digressions, dialogue, or anecdotes may obscure the purpose of the work. Under these circumstances, the group can ask questions about what part is most important to the author, what he or she wants the audience to be focused on. Then the group can help the author see which parts of the writing contribute to the purpose and which parts distract from it.

As students become more sophisticated writers, they become more aware of language, more sensitive to precision of words. As the group listens to someone read, they may notice that certain words are used over and over or that certain sentence patterns are used so rigidly that the work seems tedious. This is the time to discuss interesting verbs or to explore alternate sentence patterns.

Evaluation and growth are partners. To help students see how their writing is improving and to determine what is still to be accomplished, it is good to end every conference with some evaluative questions: What did you learn from writing this? What do you like best in the piece you've written? Is there any part of it that gave you trouble? Is there any way I can help you? What will you focus on in your revision? Such questions require reflection and consequently open the way for growth.

Summing Up the Reading-Writing Connection

Using fine literature as a springboard for their own writing gives students excellent models for interesting use of language. In fact, excellent children's literature is an ideal place to look for superior examples of all the different writing techniques. A strength of Writer's Triangle is that it capitalizes on this connection, showing children how they can develop their writing skills by observing how accomplished writers communicate ideas.

Many of today's new writing programs emphasize the importance of allowing student writing to reflect the students' own interests and ideas. Indeed, much of your students' work *should* be with topics they choose: personal narratives, subjects they wish to learn about, approaches they wish to try out. There is also a place, however, for direct teaching of skills.

We teach skills in Writer's Triangle with writing activities that focus on the specific skills students have already examined in the required literature. Within this structure, we try to give choices and allow a range of possibilities, but we believe the structure is important. By encouraging students to use techniques they might otherwise not have noticed or might have been uncomfortable trying, we enable them to increase their writing repertoires.

FORMS

- ▼ Priority List
- ▼ Grading
- ▼ Management Chart
- ▼ Sample Management Chart
- ▼ Student Discussion Self-evaluation
- ▼ End-of-Year Evaluation
- ▼ Parent Evaluation

Priority List

Number all the books to show which you want to read most and which you want to read least. Put a **1** by the book you wish to read more than any other book. Place a **2** by your second choice, a **3** by your third choice, and so on. If you have read the book before, place an **R** next to your number. Remember, a fresh reading is essential for good discussion.

Titles	Number

Grading

Students' Names	FCT	DISC	DRAFT	FINAL	AVG.	
Michael A.	90	100	100	100	97.5	
Sarah B.	90	100	75	75	85	writing 1 day late
Susan C.	80	100	100	100	95	
Joanne D.	60	100	100	100	90	great effort after poor FCT
Carolyn E.	60	0	100	100	65	
David F.	100	100	0	0	50	no writing
Jim G.	80	100	75	75	82.5	
Dana H.	90	100	50	50	72.5	
William I.	90	0	75	0	41.25	no discussion effort; no final paper

Goal = On-time participation

Fact Check Test (FCT) — 10 percent off for each wrong answer.

Discussion (DIS) — 100 percent if good participation.
0 percent if book not read.

First Draft — 100 percent if on time and shows effort.
One grade lower each day late.

Final Draft — 100 percent if on time and shows effort at improvement.
One grade lower each day late.

Writer's Triangle © 1989

Management Chart

Book Sequence_____ Room_____

Students' Names	Grades										Novel Titles							
	FCT	DISC	DRAFT	FINAL	AVG.													

Schedule

FCT

DISC

DRAFT

FINAL

Management Chart

Book Sequence ___3___   Room __14__

Students' Names	FCT	DISC	DRAFT	FINAL	AVG.		DIR	EE	GGH	HR	IE	OMF	SOB	TTD	WM	WIT
Allen	80	100	100	90	93							✓				
Bonnie	100	100	100	100	100							✓				
Charley	70	100	100	90	90							✓				
Danielle	70	90	100	90	88							✓				
Earl	100	100	100	100	100									✓		
Frances	80	100	100	100	95							✓		✓		
Georges	100	100	100	100	100											
Hermine	70	100	100	100	93							✓				
Ivan	100	100	100	100	100											✓
Jeanne	90	100	100	100	98									✓		
Karl	100	100	100	100	100									✓		
Lisa	80	100	100	100	95									✓		
Mitch	100	100	100	100	100									✓		
Nicole	100	100	100	100	100									✓		
Otto	80	100	100	100	95											✓
Paula	90	100	100	100	98							✓				
Richard	90	100	100	100	98									✓		
Shary	90	100	100	100	98							✓				
Tomas	70	100	90	100	90									✓		
Virginie	90	100	100	100	98										✓	
Walter	90	100	100	100	98										✓	
Alberto	100	100	80	100	95							✓				
Beryl	100	100	100	100	100										✓	
Chris	100	100	100	100	100										✓	
Debby	70	100	100	100	93							✓				
Ernesto	70	100	100	100	93										✓	

Novel Titles (column headers): DIR, EE, GGH, HR, IE, OMF, SOB, TTD, WM, WIT

Author names at bottom: OMF — Cooper, SOB — Lewis, WIT — Reynsfeld

Schedule

FCT	Jan. 19
DISC	Jan. 21
DRAFT	Jan. 28
FINAL	Feb. 4

Name_____ Room_____

Student Discussion Self-evaluation

While you are participating in the discussion, mark on this
line every time you make a contribution.

_____

1. Looking at my tally of contributions to the discussion, I participated

_____   _____   _____
      Often   Sometimes   Rarely

2. I used examples from the book to support my ideas

_____   _____   _____
      Often   Sometimes   Rarely

3. I stayed on the topic

_____   _____   _____
      Often   Sometimes   Rarely

4. When I didn't understand, I asked questions

_____   _____   _____
      Often   Sometimes   Rarely

5. I showed respect for others by listening, taking my turn, and not interrupting when
   others were speaking

_____   _____   _____
      Often   Sometimes   Rarely

Overall, I would rate my contributions to this discussion as

_____   _____   _____
   Outstanding in   Average   Very Weak

Name _____ Room_____

End-of-Year-Evaluation

1. Which book did you like best?
   Explain your reasons.

   _____

   _____

   _____

   _____

2. Which book did you like least?
   Explain your reasons.

   _____

   _____

   _____

   _____

3. How did the Writer's Triangle help you become:
   a. A better reader _____

   _____

   b. A better writer _____

   _____

4. What other benefits did you gain from Writer's Triangle?

   _____

   _____

   _____

5. Did you have any problems with Writer's Triangle you would like to share?

   _____

   _____

   _____

Parent Evaluation

This year your child has participated in a Reading-Writing-Listening program we call Writer's Triangle. As part of the program, students were required to read high-quality children's novels, listen to books read aloud by their teachers, and view literature filmstrips. Each of these experiences included a related writing assignment.

To help us improve and refine this program, we would appreciate it if you would take a few minutes to complete the following evaluation and return it to school by_____ .

	Very Much	Somewhat	Not At All
1. My child enjoyed participating in Writer's Triangle.	_____	_____	_____
2. My child has been reading more this year.	_____	_____	_____
3. My child has developed more sophistication in reading.	_____	_____	_____
4. My child has shown growth in interpreting literature.	_____	_____	_____
5. My child has become more interested in writing.	_____	_____	_____
6. My child has become a more fluent writer.	_____	_____	_____
7. This program has made my child more prepared for coping with the longer assignments and independent requirements of secondary school.	_____	_____	_____

8.   Other comments. _____

_____

_____

Book Annotations

1. The Dark Is Rising

Will Stanton discovers that he is something other than an ordinary English boy. He has been destined from birth to be one of the Old Ones, immortal keepers of the Light, who have struggled for thousands of years against the forces of evil, the Dark. Will is plunged at once into a quest for the six magical signs that will one day aid the Old Ones in their battle between the Dark and the Light. Life for Will becomes strangely wonderful as he is drawn through terror and delight.

2. The 18th Emergency

When Marv Hammerman catches Benjie writing his name on the chart near the Neanderthal man, Benjie's life becomes one of terror. There is no question about it, Marv is going to get him! Both funny and realistic, the story moves quickly as we read to see how Benjie will survive this "terrible" threat.

3. The Great Gilly Hopkins

Gilly is a foster child who has been bouncing from family to family. She is highly intelligent, enormously angry, and determined to contact her real mother, whom she fantasizes will make her whole life fine. As the book opens, she is being taken to her new placement with huge, untidy Maime Trotter. Trotter is as determined to love and help Gilly as Gilly is to rebel. Things do work out, but not the way anyone would have expected.

4. Hazel Rye

Hazel Rye can barely read or write and has failed sixth grade. This doesn't bother her father, however. His education is no better than hers, and he has plenty of money to take her out to dinner all the time and buy a big Cadillac to drive her around. She daydreams about quitting school so she can drive a taxi and make $300 a week. She'd also like to fix up her run-down orange grove and then sell it for lots of money. When Felder Poole and his family arrive in town, it looks as if her dream may come true. Instead, with his own ideas about the grove, Felder shakes the foundations of Hazel's world.

5. Ida Early Comes Over the Mountain

The Sutton children have lost their mother and are being cared for by bossy, overbearing Aunt Earnestine when Ida Early arrives on their doorstep looking for work. Tall and homely, with a warm, generous spirit and a quick laugh, she brings joy back into the house. She brings joy to her readers too, as we laugh with this backwoods Mary Poppins who tells tall stories, delights in games, and manages to get her way with the children's obnoxious aunts.

6. One-eyed Cat

Ned Wallis receives a gun for his birthday. He sneaks it out one night and shoots at a moving shadow. Later, when he sees a one-eyed cat in the neighborhood, he is sure he is responsible for its injury. How Ned works through his guilt and fear about the cat and how he copes with Mrs. Scallop, his awful housekeeper, makes an intense and riveting story.

7. One More Flight

Eleven-year-old Dobby has run away again from the Residential Treatment Center, where troubled kids live and wait to be placed in foster homes. He has run away nine times in his life and this time, if he gets caught, he'll be sent to juvenile hall. Rescued by an older boy who rehabilitates injured eagles and hawks and returns them to the wild, Dobby discovers what freedom really means.

8. Sign of the Beaver

Pioneering in the Maine woods in 1786, twelve-year- old Matt is waiting for his father to bring the rest of the family to their new home. After Matt is almost killed by a swarm of bees, he is befriended by an Indian boy and his grandfather, who teach him how to survive in the wilderness. Matt's struggle to become a true woodsman and to earn the respect of the Indians keeps the story exciting.

9. This Time of Darkness

Amy lives in the future, in an underground labyrinth of tunnels and corridors, the lower level of a domed city. Life is bleak and boring, and when the boy, Axel, claims to have come from the "outside," she believes him. Together, they plan their escape back to his people. Exciting, dramatic, and frightening, this book is a stimulating and creative exploration of what could be in store for Earth.

10. Tuck Everlasting

When Winnie Foster runs off to the wood behind her house, she meets the Tucks, who have found a spring that has given them eternal life. They beg her to keep their secret. If people learn of it, the world will never be the same. Winnie agrees, but it is not so simple. Someone already knows and has a dreadful plan to use the water to make himself rich and powerful! At the end only Winnie can help the Tucks, and to do so she must make some difficult decisions.

11. The White Mountains

Will lives in a future time when technology has reverted to a primitive state. No longer are there any cities, so people live in small, rural villages. The world has been taken over by Tripods, which take young people at age 13 and "cap" them so that they can be controlled. When Will learns about a stronghold of freedom in the White Mountains, he and his cousin run off to find it. Will they be able to get there before the Tripods catch up with them, or will they be caught and capped, forever prisoners of the menacing Tripods? Their race through three countries makes for an exciting and dramatic story.

12. Words by Heart

It is 1910, and Lena Sills and her family have left Scattercreek, their comfortable southern black community, to try to better themselves out west. Possessed of a "magic mind," Lena wins a contest for reciting Bible verses, but her success also wins some enemies. So does her father's hard work and success in pleasing Mrs. Chism, his boss. This powerful book explores risk and courage, hate and love, ignorance and understanding as is shows us a picture of life for a black family struggling to maintain dignity in a hostile environment.

13. A Wrinkle in Time

Meg, alone with her brother and a friend, is transported to another world by three extraterrestrial beings so that she can search for her father, who is missing. He has been doing secret work on tesseracts, or wrinkles in time, and the only way to follow him is to travel as he did through these "wrinkles." In their courageous quest, the children face awesome and terrifying experiences and discover strengths in themselves they did not know they had.

FILMSTRIPS

▼ Call It Courage

▼ The Golden Goblet

▼ The House of Dies Drear

▼ The Tombs of Atuan

Call It Courage

Filmstrip set (Cat. #394-76962-7) is available from Random House Media, Dept. 437, 400 Hahn Road, Westminster, MD 21157-9939. It is based on the book *Call It Courage,* by Sperry Armstrong (MacMillan, 1968, ISBN 0-02-786030-2). Historical Fiction.

Summary: Mafatu, the Polynesian boy, is afraid of the sea. When he was a young child, the sea claimed his mother, and he has never overcome his fear. The other boys mock him and his father is ashamed. One day he decides to go off to a distant island to learn to conquer his terror. Bringing Uri, his dog, and followed by Kivi, the albatross, he sets out. During his time of trial he faces a wild boar, a shark, an octopus, man-eating men, and of course the sea. He returns home a hero.

Comments: An extraordinary story, beautifully written with a simple, direct plot, *Call It Courage* offers us a look at ourselves through the eyes of an ancient culture. The simplicity of the story makes it a good choice to use in film version. The design and fine artwork of the film adds another dimension to this classic story.

Name _____ Room _____

Call It Courage

by Armstrong Sperry

Meet with your discussion group before watching the filmstrip and talk about what might frighten you so much it could keep you from doing something you really wanted to do.

As you watch and listen, think about

▌ how, in Part One, Sperry helps us sympathize with Mafatu's fear
▌ how, in Part Two, the artist intensifies our response by using colors and lines that support Sperry's story
▌ what sound effects make the story come alive for you

Schedule

Part One _____

Part Two _____

First Draft Due _____

Final Draft Due _____

Notes

_____

_____

_____

_____

_____

Writer's Triangle © 1989

Call It Courage
by Armstrong Sperry

Part One

1. **Throughout this part of the story, Mafatu is torn by the conflict within him. This comes from the clash of incompatible feelings and needs. What is this conflict that torments Mafatu?**

   He is terrified of the sea, yet he knows he must be brave to be a respected fisherman and warrior.

2. **Why does Sperry begin his story with an introduction that tells us about the ancient Polynesian people?**

   Sperry prepares us for understanding the people in the story. He explains why courage is essential in their culture. He also foreshadows the end by telling us that this is a survival story with a successful outcome that inspired others for generations.

3. **All his growing years, Mafatu has been an outsider. He has been lonely but has made the best of things with his animal friends. Why, suddenly, does he feel the need to go off alone to try to prove himself?**

   As the boys his age are reaching manhood and preparing to take their place in society, Mafatu is still doing women's work and cannot participate as an equal. The situation becomes intolerable when he hears his friends speak about him in a contemptuous way.

4. **What do you think Sperry will have happen in Part Two?**

   Answers will vary but should include the idea that Mafatu will have adventures that test and prove his courage. Let the group predict whether Mafatu will ever find his way home. The clue they have is that in the introduction we are told that his people still tell stories of his bravery.

Part Two

1. **Sperry equips Mafatu with certain survival skills. We see some of them in the first part of the story, although we may not recognize them as survival skills at the time. What are some of these experiences and skills that help Mafatu survive alone on the forbidden island?**

He learns how to handle and build tools and utensils. These skills which are the work of women, not warriors, turn out to be very useful. He also knows how to hunt and gather food, treat an injury, and build a sail canoe. In addition, memories of his grandfather's stories alert him to the danger he may face from the men of the smoking island.

2. **How do you think your understanding of _Call It Courage_ was enhanced by the pictures and sound effects of the filmstrip?**

The answers will vary but may include ideas similar to the following:

▌ In his pictures, the colors the artist uses give us a sense of life on a primitive jungle island. The artist makes us feel things through his use of lines and colors. We feel violence when we see jagged clashing lines and colors. We feel desolate when Mafatu is sailing on the flat, glassy, empty sea. We feel joy at the final glorious sunburst. The pictures reflect Sperry's poetic language. We can literally see the jungle trees close in, as if to imprison Mafatu. When Sperry says there is a fan of light, the artist makes it appear in the filmstrip.

▌ The sound effects of the filmstrip help, too. We don't have to imagine the sounds of the jungle creatures and the frightening drums—we can hear them. We hear the sounds of the storm and the cool trickle of a freshwater stream when Mafatu is thirsty.

Writer's Triangle © 1989

3. **Adventure stories, whether they are realistic or fantastic, are always exciting. How would you classify Mafatu's adventures? Is Sperry's book a fantasy or a story that could have happened to a real boy?**

Answers will vary. However, they might include the following:

■ The beliefs and customs of the early Polynesian people are portrayed accurately.

■ Sperry builds a background for Mafatu that gives him the skills to survive.

■ The adventures themselves are things a person on such an island might have encountered. Mafatu does not need magic powers to return home as a warrior.

■ While it might seem impossible for Mafatu to have found his way in the vast sea, we should remember that the early Polynesian people who settled these islands and traveled between them did just that.

Call It Courage
by Armstrong Sperry

CHOOSE ONE WRITING ACTIVITY THAT INTERESTS YOU.

A. Write an adventure story in which your character tests himself or herself against nature. Set it in your own time period so that you can make all the events believable. When you set up the problem, make sure your character has the skills he or she needs. Your hero or heroine must have a specific goal to reach. This may be rescuing someone or surviving in a harsh environment or in a natural disaster.

B. In *Call It Courage*, Sperry keeps us interested by creating an exciting problem. However, a book can't be all intense danger. We'd get tired of it and might stop finding it exciting. To keep this from happening, Sperry varies the pace of his story by having Mafatu have periods in which he has fun and enjoys his surroundings. Write an extension of Sperry's story. Pretend you are Mafatu twenty years after *Call It Courage* ended. You are now chief of your people. The eaters of men are coming to invade your island. You must be a resourceful leader to help your people survive. Vary the pace of your story, alternating between fear and relief and between danger and success to maintain reader interest.

Writer's Triangle © 1989

The Golden Goblet

Filmstrip set (Cat. #394-76994-5) is available from Random House Media, Dept. 437, 400 Hahn Road, Westminster, MD 21157-9939. It is based on the book (available only in paperback) *The Golden Goblet,* **by Eloise Jarvis McGraw (Penguin/Puffin, 1986, ISBN 0-14-030335-0).** Historical Fiction/Mystery.

Summary: When an Egyptian boy, Ranofer, loses his father, his cruel half brother, Gebu, becomes his guardian, and his dream of becoming a goldsmith is shattered—Gebu will not apprentice him to a goldsmith. When Ranofer discovers that Gebu is involved in a scheme to steal gold, he is forced to be an apprentice in Gebu's stonecutting shop. Then Ranofer discovers another theft, that of a beautiful golden goblet, and the plot thickens. With the help of his friend, Heqet, and an old man, he unravels the secret of how Gebu is robbing tombs and paves the way for a happier future for himself.

Comments: A satisfying and interesting mystery set in ancient Egypt, *The Golden Goblet* moves quickly and offers interesting historical information.

Name _____ Room _____

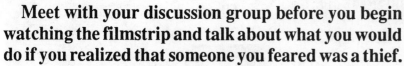

Pre-Viewing Focus

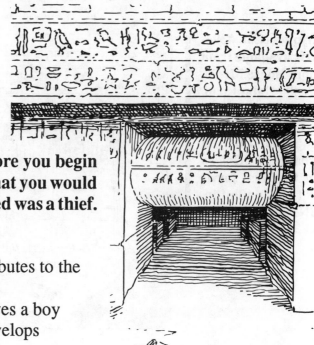

The Golden Goblet
by Eloise McGraw

Meet with your discussion group before you begin watching the filmstrip and talk about what you would do if you realized that someone you feared was a thief.

As you watch and listen, think about

- how the setting of ancient Egypt contributes to the story
- how the author, Eloise McGraw, involves a boy your age in a mystery, and how she develops suspense about how it will be resolved.

Schedule

Part One _____

Part Two _____

First Draft Due _____

Final Draft Due _____

Notes

_____

_____

_____

_____

_____

Writer's Triangle © 1989

Filmstrip Discussion Guide

The Golden Goblet
by Eloise McGraw

Part One

SETTING

Why did McGraw set this story in ancient Egypt?

The setting creates interest and teaches us about the period. There are things in ancient Egypt we don't have: goldsmiths with apprentices, wineskins, and papyrus gatherers. This lets her tell a story she couldn't tell in a modern setting.

PLOT

What is the main conflict in the story?

The conflict is between Ranofer and Gebu, Ranofer's half brother. Gebu mistreats him and doesn't let him follow his strong desire to work with gold.

CHARACTER

What does Ranofer's inner conflict about being an unwitting thief tell us about Ranofer?

He is honest. He is willing to risk Gebu's wrath to defend his principles. He cares about being a good worker and wants to be well thought of in the goldsmith's shop.

PLOT PREDICTION

McGraw has set up the story now. What must she have happen in the second half?

Gebu, who we know is a bad person must be exposed. We need to know what dishonest things he's doing. Ranofer is the hero. Like all heroes, he must do something heroic, and he must get rewarded or at least come up a winner.

Part Two

PLOT

What clues did we get throughout the filmstrip that Gebu might be a tomb robber?

We saw (1) tomb robbers being executed in Part One, (2) Gebu's increasing and unexplained wealth, (3) Ranofer's discovery in the stonecutter's workshop of the scroll showing the tomb's secret room, and (4) Ranofer's finding the golden goblet in Gebu's room.

CHARACTER

1. How does Gebu's nasty personality lead to his being caught?

Gebu's cruelty to Ranofer makes him Ranofer's enemy. If Gebu hadn't been so hostile, Ranofer would be off minding his own business as a goldsmith's apprentice.

2. What does Ranofer's request for a reward show us about Ranofer?

He's not greedy. His original goal is still what he wants: a reasonable way to have a successful life.

MOOD

How does McGraw create suspense in this story?

McGraw keeps putting obstacles in Ranofer's way. At each part we are unsure of how he will get around them.

1. She makes him a stonecutter's apprentice when he wants to be a goldsmith.

2. Ranofer can't learn from the master who was a friend of his father, because his days are occupied.

3. Ranofer can't discover what Gebu is doing even when he spies on Gebu.

4. Ranofer can't convince the people in the palace about Gebu robbing the tomb until the dwarf intervenes.

Writer's Triangle © 1989

Writing Activity

The Golden Goblet

by Eloise McGraw

CHOOSE ONE WRITING ACTIVITY THAT INTERESTS YOU.

A. In a mystery book, plot is always an important focus and must be well thought-out before the writer begins. Otherwise, the writer can end up with a confused story or even with a story that has no solution. The plot of a mystery story always involves some secret. Uncovering the secret is the task of the hero or heroine of the book. The secret can be a crime. For example, in *The Golden Goblet* Gebu steals treasures from the tombs. Or the secret can be a hidden room in a house, a treasure, or information contained in an important letter or document.

   The first task of a mystery writer is to decide what the secret of the book will be. The second is to decide how it will come to the attention of the hero or heroine; that is, to decide how the secret will become a problem. The third task is to plan how the hero will uncover the secret. This is the solution to the mystery. Once these basic plans are made, the writer has to plant clues to the solution of the mystery and decide how these clues will come into the story. Use the attached plot form to plan your mystery. After your teacher approves your plans, use the information on your form to write an interesting, suspenseful mystery story.

B. Eloise McGraw had to do a lot of research about ancient Egypt in order to write *The Golden Goblet*. She had to know about an ancient Egyptian goldsmith's shop, she had to know about Egyptian tombs, and she had to know about the dress and customs of the time. If you wanted to set a story in a time other than your own, you would have to do this kind of research too.

   Choose a setting from an earlier period for a story you might like to write. A house in ancient Rome, a medieval castle, or an Indian teepee on the Great Plains are possible settings for you to consider, although you may choose another if you prefer. Do research about the setting of your choice, and then write an opening scene from a book. Have your main character walk into the setting you've chosen and look around. Using his or her point of view, write what is seen, heard, or smelled and what might be going on in your setting. Include many details, for it is details that will make your setting seem authentic.

Mystery Plot Form

The Golden Goblet

by Eloise McGraw

1. Your secret or problem:

_____

_____

_____

2. How the secret becomes a problem for your hero or heroine:

_____

_____

_____

3. How the hero or heroine uncovers the secret or solves the problem:

_____

_____

_____

4. Clues to help the hero or heroine:

_____

_____

_____

5. Important people in your mystery other than the hero or heroine
   (who are they and what role do they play? for example, who is your
   villain? does anyone help your hero or heroine? is there a victim?):

_____

_____

_____

Writer's Triangle © 1989

The House of Dies Drear

Filmstrip is available from Pied Piper Media, 1645 Monrovia Avenue, Costa Mesa, CA 92627. It is based on the book, *The House of Dies Drear*, by Virginia Hamilton (Macmillan, 1968, ISBN 0-02-742500-2). Mystery.

Summary: The House of Dies Drear was an Ohio station on the Underground Railroad. It is filled with secret tunnels and sliding panels, and when Thomas Small and his family come there to live, they discover that it is also filled with odd sounds and mysterious happenings. One of the mysteries is Mr. Pluto, the caretaker, who, it turns out, has discovered the treasure of Dies Drear and is protecting it from the neighboring Darrows. In the end, Thomas's historian-father agrees to keep the treasure room a secret until he can inventory all the items for the foundation that supervises the house.

Comments: This short, one-part film lesson is exciting because of all the ghosts, mysterious events, and sneaking around in dark tunnels. It can be a good introduction to further reading about the Underground Railroad.

Pre-Viewing Focus

The House of Dies Drear

by Virginia Hamilton

Meet with your discussion group before you begin watching the filmstrip and talk about how you, if you had lived in the early 1880s, might have hidden some runaway slaves who came to your house on their way north.

As you watch and listen, think about

▮ how Virginia Hamilton creates an air of mystery in her story

▮ what Hamilton wants the readers to learn about while they enjoy their story

Schedule

Filmstrip Viewing _____

First Draft Due _____

Final Draft Due _____

Notes

_____

_____

_____

_____

_____

_____

Writer's Triangle © 1989

The House of Dies Drear

by Virginia Hamilton

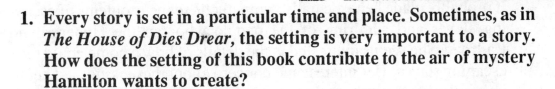

1. **Every story is set in a particular time and place. Sometimes, as in *The House of Dies Drear,* the setting is very important to a story. How does the setting of this book contribute to the air of mystery Hamilton wants to create?**

   The house is old and looks "forbidding and mysterious." It has secret passages and secret sliding panels. Thomas hears an odd breathing sound after he tumbles into the secret passage. There is a lot of history connected with the house, and a superstitious person could think about ghosts in connection with it.

2. **How does Hamilton let the readers of her story know that it is real villains, not ghosts, who are making things happen in the story?**

   She focuses our attention on the Darrows, who are big, frowning, and tough. Even young Mac Darrow is threatening and frightens Thomas when he first meets him. Thomas's father is always a practical voice in the story. Thomas may believe at times that he has encountered a supernatural being, but his father seems to know that the answer to their mysteries is either with Mr. Pluto or the Darrows.

3. **Every mystery has some sort of secret. Uncovering the secret is usually the basis for the plot of the story. What is the secret of *The House of Dies Drear?***

   Dies Drear had a treasure, which Mr. Pluto and his son are protecting and which the Darrows are trying to find.

4. **Mystery writers give readers clues to the secrets in their story. What clues does Hamilton give us that there is more than one man being Pluto?**

   Pluto seemed strong and healthy when he chased Thomas, but he was supposed to be sick. Sometimes he wore heavy hide gloves, which made Thomas's father think he'd burned his hands. But at other times his hands were bare. Mr. Small said this was mysterious. When the family first met Pluto, he stood where there was the least light, behaved strangely, and left fast. Yet, Mr. Small said he was not so strange when he'd met him before. Finally, the day after Mr. Pluto came into their kitchen, he greeted Thomas and his family and welcomed them as though he'd never seen them.

5. **Virginia Hamilton was born in an Ohio town that had once been a station on the Underground Railroad. Her own grandfather was a runaway slave. How do you think this history influenced her writing?**

It probably made her especially sympathetic to the problems of escaping slaves and admiring of the people who ran the Underground Railroad. She seems interested in the details of how a home could hide escaping slaves. Her interest and concern about these issues led her to write a story about them that could teach today's children about this time and these events.

6. **Mayhew says, "We wear the mask that grins and lies." What does he mean by these words?**

Literally, of course, he has been fooling people by wearing a mask. But if we look for deeper meaning, we might also say that any time people pretend to be what they are not, they are wearing a mask. There has been a lot of pretending or lying going on in this story. Dies Drear pretended in order to help slaves escape. Pluto has been lying and pretending in order to protect the treasure. The Darrows are sneaking around and hiding their real reasons for wanting the Smalls to get out of the house. We might also think that a grinning face can mask other, deeper feelings.

The House of Dies Drear

by Virginia Hamilton

CHOOSE ONE WRITING ACTIVITY THAT INTERESTS YOU.

A. Writers often have to do background research before they write a book. At the core of this story is Virginia Hamilton's interest in the Underground Railroad. Research this topic in an encyclopedia or history book as if you were planning to use it in a book you were going to write. Put the information you find together, telling the history of the Underground Railroad in this country prior to the Civil War. Include any interesting facts and personal stories you find that would help you make your book exciting to read.

B. Pretend you are a runaway slave. You have been on the run for several days, moving at night, hiding by day. Your store of food is now gone and you are near exhaustion. Your only hope is the "safe" farmhouse ahead of you that someone told you about before you left home. It is a station on the Underground Railroad. Describe the experiences you have from the time you approach the house until the people there get you on your way again. Be sure to include descriptions of your surroundings, the people you meet, and your feelings.

Writer's Triangle © 1989

The Tombs of Atuan

Filmstrip set (Cat. #394-77155-9) is available from Random House Media, Dept. 437, 400 Hahn Road, Westminster, MD 21157-9939. It is based on the book *The Tombs of Atuan,* by Ursula LeGuin (Atheneum, 1971, ISBN 0-689-20680-1; in paperback, Bantam, 1975, ISBN 0-553-14946-6). Fantasy.

Summary: As a young child, Tenar was chosen to become Arha and replace the dead priestess of the Tombs of Atuan. Although she has great power, her life is basically dull and lonely. Thar and Kossil teach her to fulfill her role, which includes ruling the vast underground labyrinth that contains their treasure.

One day Ged the magician comes seeking the Ring of Erreth-Akbe, a powerful object that can restore peace in his land. Normally, anyone seeking this treasure becomes trapped in the dark, twisting tunnels and will either be executed or die of thirst and starvation. Arha was responsible for the deaths of three prisoners, a fact that still upsets her. When Ged shows her that she has choices and possibilities, she helps him escape.

Comments: This is a serious story, suitable for mature students. It is a fantasy that carries a mood of power and terror and encourages the reader or viewer to think about issues such as blind obedience and decision making.

Name _____ Room _____

The Tombs of Atuan
by Ursula LeGuin

Meet with your discussion group before you begin watching the filmstrip and talk about whether you would rather be a regular kid or a person with immense powers who had to live apart from everyone else.

As you watch and listen, think about

▮ how Ursula LeGuin creates a mood of terror
▮ which things in this story are possible and which could happen only in a fantasy

Schedule

Part One _____

Part Two _____

First Draft Due _____

Final Draft Due _____

Notes

_____

_____

_____

_____

_____

Writer's Triangle © 1989

The Tombs of Atuan

by Ursula LeGuin

Part One

1. How does the author create a mood of terror in the story?

We feel the unreliability of superstition and secrets and Arha's isolation from a normal, safe world and common people. Along with Arha, we are afraid of the unknown: the Nameless Ones, the untold mysteries, the unexplored and dark labyrinth. We are worried that Arha might lose her way and not be able to return. It is especially scary because she must go underground alone.

2. *The Tombs of Atuan* is a fantasy. LeGuin made up the whole story, including the setting. Some things seem real, however. Based on what you know about early civilizations, which parts of the story seem realistic?

Some early societies had god-kings. Some religions had priestesses and elaborate temples. People used to make sacrifices to their gods. Ancient labyrinths have been discovered by archaeologists in Egypt and Crete. The people—Arha, Maran, Thar, and Kossil—behave the way we'd expect people from such societies to behave.

3. Arha gives the order to have the prisoners killed, which upsets her enormously. How does her distress change her so that the direction of the story changes?

She is so upset that she begins to question her role as High Priestess. This turning point in the story hints to the reader that Arha will no longer blindly accept everything Kossil and Thar tell her.

4. What is Kossil's role in the story?

She is the villain of the story. Supposedly Arha's teacher and friend, she really is more interested in her own power and the god-king she serves.

5. What do you think LeGuin will have happen in Part 2?

Arha will have to make a decision about the new prisoner she trapped. We might also guess that there will be a confrontation between Kossil and Arha.

Part Two

1. **Pretend you are Arha before she meets Ged. Do you like being High Priestess? Think about the things that are good about your life and the things you've had to give up.**

Answers will vary, but may include:

A. The main thing Arha has going in her life is that she is permanently taken care of and has enormous power and control in her little world.

B. In order to be High Priestess, she must put up with loneliness and isolation and a dull daily existence. She has no chance to wear pretty clothes or to have fun and no chance of having her own family.

2. **What does Ged do that makes Arha join forces with him?**

He shows her a different view of herself. He does this with his magic illusions and by knowing her name. This shows her she has choices and possibilities. She can act as Arha, the High Priestess, or she can behave as Tenar, the girl. At this point she begins to understand that she has choices. She puts on an act for the listening Kossil and from then on helps Ged.

3. **The Tombs of Atuan are swallowed by an earthquake near the end of the story. On one level this provides excitement and adventure. There is a deeper meaning, however. What do you think the collapse of the tombs might represent to Tenar/Arha?**

The tombs represent all the beliefs she used to have. They also stand for the way she lived and behaved as High Priestess. She puts this behind her when she agrees to go with Ged, and the collapse of the tombs is a final, physical end to this part of her life.

Writing Activity ◤

The Tombs of Atuan
by Ursula LeGuin

CHOOSE ONE WRITING ACTIVITY THAT INTERESTS YOU.

A.   Fantasy stories sometimes have a magic object that has power
only under certain conditions. In *The Tombs of Atuan* the magic
Ring of Erreth-Akbe was powerful only when it was whole. When
it was broken, there was war and hatred. Peace existed only when
it was together.

Write a story in which you create a magic object that has power
only under a special condition. This condition can be wholeness,
as it is for the Ring of Erreth-Akbe, or it can be a time of year or
possession by a certain person or some other circumstance of your
choosing.

B.   The labyrinth (maze) in *The Tombs of Atuan* plays a very
important role in the story. It is made into a frightening and
mysterious place because it is underground, unlighted, and full of
dangerous places. That only a few chosen people are allowed in
the labyrinth adds to the atmosphere of terror that surrounds it.

Pretend you are trapped in the labyrinth of the Tombs of Atuan.
Tell why you are there, how you got in, and what it feels like to be
groping for a way out. Continue your story, showing what happens
to you in the labyrinth and how you get out. Try to make your
experience different from the one Ged had.

READ-ALOUDS

- ▲ Eight Mules from Monterey
- ▲ Indian in the Cupboard
- ▲ Night Journeys
- ▲ Sarah Bishop

Eight Mules from Monterey

**by Patricia Beatty
(Morrow, 1982,
ISBN 0-688-01047-4;
not available in paperback).
Historical Fiction.**

Summary: Fayette Ashmore is the heroine of this story in which she and her younger brother accompany their mother, a newly trained but jobless librarian, into the California mountains to bring books to the mountain people. Their motivation is their need for money, created by the death of their father and Mrs. Ashmore's reluctance to solve this problem by marrying Mr. Herbert. The year is 1916, so Mrs. Ashmore's determination to fend for herself shows a lot of independence and spunk. They travel on mules—hence the title—and begin with a whiskey-drinking mule skinner as their guide. When drunk, he cuts himself badly with an axe, and they continue with a hermit woodsman. They make it to their goal, but not before burying a mountain boy who died of typhoid and meeting up with moonshiners, who get their guide drunk. The issues of drinking and moonshine are not dominant in the book, but they do provide some humor and action.

Comments: Although the heroine is a girl, the story with its mules and moonshiners appeals equally to boys. Interesting as well as unusual historical information is presented without being didactic. Some of the events—such as teetotalers smashing liquor bottles, moonshiners shooting at people, and women faced with the prospect of marrying for money and security—can provide good material for discussion of moral issues.

Prelistening Focus

Eight Mules from Monterey
by Patricia Beatty

Meet with your discussion group before the book is begun and talk about what kinds of books you would bring to isolated mountain people if you were a librarian who was determined to offer these people the services of a library.

As you listen to the story, think about

■ how Patricia Beatty uses humor to make her story enjoyable

■ what parts of the book might be based on true incidents (at the end of the book, Beatty tells the reader what is real and what is fiction)

Schedule

Book Will Be Finished by _____

First Draft Due _____

Final Draft Due _____

Notes

_____

_____

_____

_____

_____

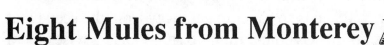

Discussion Guide

Eight Mules from Monterey

by Patricia Beatty

Chapter 1

In the first chapter of a book, authors try to introduce major characters and let readers know something of the problems the characters face; that is, they introduce the plot and give us a glimpse of the action that will move the book along.

1. What has Beatty let us know about Fayette?

She's headstrong and spunky, as demonstrated by her lies to the Hillman sisters and her request to Mrs. Wallace to intercede with Mr. Wallace on her mother's behalf.

2. What has Beatty let us know about Mrs. Ashmore?

She's courageous and adventurous, which we see by her willingness to deliver books to the mountain people with a mule team. She's independent and unwilling to marry just for security.

3. What do we know of their problem?

Mrs. Ashmore is widowed and needs money, a problem that affects the whole family. It is hard to get a job as a librarian, so she plans to prove herself by establishing a network of library outposts in the mountains.

Chapter 2

One way an author makes a book enjoyable is to give the reader hints about what is to come. By giving us well-placed clues about events that will happen later, the author allows us to anticipate them. This can heighten suspense or pleasure.

1. What clues does Beatty sprinkle throughout Chapter 2 that alert the reader to the possibility that the Ashmores may find the journey up the mountain more difficult than they anticipated?

Mrs. Ashmore shows her own uncertainty when she frowns at the image of herself in a man's felt hat (p. 35). Mr. Wallace is negative about the mountain people, who he says are generally not interested in books (p. 36). Mr. Wallace is so eager to get away from the scene that he leaves the motor of his Overland running (p. 39). He advises them about telegraph lines and mail service in case of "insurmountable troubles" (p. 39). Mr. Wallace doesn't like the idea of guiding a woman and her children, and his behavior generally indicates a lack of helpfulness. He has provided the family with mules to ride, when they expected horses, and they have trouble handling the mules. Even Fayette has doubts about whether she was wise to push Mrs. Wallace into getting her mother the job.

2. **How do the things that alert us to the Ashmores' upcoming difficulties make us think the book will probably be more humorous than suspenseful?**

Mr. Wallace seems somewhat fussy, which is a humorous trait. Mr. Murfree is an odd, amusing character. He is unpleasant, but there is nothing sinister about him. We are amused at the problems the Ashmores have with the mules. There is, after all, something absurd about the picture of someone trying to control a mule.

Chapter 3

Patricia Beatty accomplishes three things in this chapter. She injects humor into her story; she introduces us to the kind of people the library will be serving; and she gives the plot a sharp twist.

1. **What is amusing in this chapter?**

Murfree turns out to be a whiskey drinker, and Beatty sets up a conflict between him and all the women in the story. He is punished for drinking when he cuts his foot and Malindy shoots all his whiskey bottles. We also learn how he escaped getting married, which makes him something of a comic character.

2. **How does meeting the Mackenzies give us a clue to the nature of the people Mrs. Ashmore's library will be serving?**

We see that they are nearly illiterate. They are willing to be a library outpost, however, asking to be provided with picture books.

Writer's Triangle © 1989

3. What is the sharp twist in the story?

Mr. Murfree cannot continue the journey. They will have to have a new muleteer, possibly someone called the Possum.

Chapter 4

In this chapter we are introduced to Mr. Turlock, a complex, interesting character. Beatty makes us interested in him by having the Ashmores, especially Fayette, distrust him and at the same time having Mr. Turlock be a sympathetic character.

1. What things make Mr. Turlock seem dangerous or untrustworthy?

He looks rather wild and strange. He lives in the wild and stays away from people. He isn't communicative, and there seems to be a secret about him. We are reminded of this by the Picketts.

2. What information does Beatty include that makes us sympathetic to him?

He is gentle and doesn't want to kill animals. He is thoughtful about protecting the porcupines. He loves nature and likes to be out of doors. He even likes to read books about nature. He generally seems responsible and kind, and we feel sorry for him when we learn that his family was killed.

Chapter 5

In this chapter we meet two mountain families. Although they are very different from each other, Beatty has created a shocking problem in each household.

1. How does Beatty make us feel sympathy for Joshua Drucker?

Joshua is an orphan who is living with incredibly stingy and mean people. They won't even let him borrow books, although he wants to read. When asked if he likes living in the mountains, he looks sad and shakes his head. He seems very skinny to Fayette, which makes him sound underfed. In spite of his unhappy situation, he seems intelligent and is helpful and friendly to the Ashmores.

2. Why do you think Patricia Beatty has included the scene with the family infected with typhoid fever?

The scene shows the dangers of isolation on the mountains—the man couldn't get help for his family. It is dramatic and captures our interest. It also turns our attention from Turlock and enables Beatty to prolong the suspense about what his secret is.

Writer's Triangle © 1989

Chapter 6

Sometimes when there is a quote or saying in a book, our understanding of the saying can enlarge our understanding of the book or of a major idea in it. Beatty uses such a saying in this chapter. After Mrs. Ashmore fires Mr. Turlock, he shouts, "A pet wolf keeps coyotes away!"

1. What does he mean when he says this?

He means that he is the pet wolf who keeps other, more serious dangers at bay.

2. How might his presence have already helped them?

Apart from his skill as a muleteer and woodsman guiding them up the mountain, his presence may also have saved them from unpleasantness with the moonshiners. Because he knew them and drank with them, they basically left the Ashmores alone.

3. How might his leaving affect their future?

Without their "pet wolf," they may run into trouble they are not able to handle.

Chapter 7

Although the Ashmores run into a lot of trouble without Mr. Turlock, Beatty is careful to keep the tone of the book light. She does this by writing about their troubles in a funny way and by bringing Mr. Turlock back to them.

1. How did Beatty make their troubles amusing?

Hagar's sickness was serious, of course, but they "cured" her with some of Murfree's whiskey and she got drunk. The mule's falling was also serious, but once we knew he wasn't really hurt, we were free to enjoy the image of a mule being hoisted up the side of a ravine.

2. How does Beatty use the events of this chapter to show us about Mr. Turlock's character and his importance to the Ashmores?

Mr. Turlock's staying with them even after he was fired shows that he is responsible and good-hearted. We are further impressed with his character when he apologizes for upsetting Mrs. Ashmore and promises not to drink again. By now, everyone knows what Mr. Turlock knew all along: his services are critical to them. The Ashmores are not skilled enough in the woods to make their way up the mountain without a guide.

Chapter 8

1. **Good writers do not have stray elements floating around a story. If something is in the book, the author has a reason: either it moves the plot along, distracts us when we need to be distracted, or shows us something about the characters. Why do you think Beatty has included the Poe book in her story?**

   It is a humorous, repetitive element that helps to unify different scenes in the book. After a while we begin to anticipate that the Poe book won't "be got rid of" and enjoy seeing the various ways it finds its way back to Fayette. Her belief that the Poe book is a "hoodoo" also shows us that Fayette has some anxieties about the whole trip.

2. **One of the marks of a good book is that its main characters grow; that is, they learn something and are changed as a result. What does Beatty have Fayette learn in the course of *Eight Mules to Monterey?***

   Her experience with Mr. Turlock teaches her not to judge people too quickly nor to judge them by outward appearances. Tackling new and difficult tasks successfully teaches her to be more confident and to think of ways to take care of herself if and when she might have to.

Author's Note

Before reading the Author's Note, remind students of the Prelistening Focus question about which parts of the book are based on fact. Discuss this now. After students have all had an opportunity to share their ideas, read the Author's Note. Once this has been read, encourage students to tell if they were surprised to learn that any particular part was based on fact.

Eight Mules from Monterey

by Patricia Beatty

CHOOSE ONE WRITING ACTIVITY THAT INTERESTS YOU.

A. In some ways, all fiction is based on fact. Characters in books are often composites of people the author has met. Incidents from the author's life may find their way into a book, or an article in a newspaper may spark an idea. Even if all the incidents are made up, the author uses what he or she knows about the way things happen and the way people behave to make the book seem real.

In *Eight Mules from Monterey*, Beatty used some actual incidents she had heard about and did a little research to find out more about her topic. Then she combined this factual information with ideas from her imagination. The result is an entertaining and believable book.

Choose a real incident from your own life. It can be an exciting or dramatic one, but it doesn't have to be. It can be a simple one, such as meeting someone or finding something or learning to do something. Once you have picked an incident to write about, fictionalize it; that is, make it happen to an imaginary character. You may change things to make it work better if you like. For example, you can change the age or sex of your character. You can change the way something happened. The point is to see how you can use incidents from your own life to create interesting fiction.

B. Although Beatty's book is about the adventures of Fayette Ashmore and her family, there are many other interesting characters in the story. Joshua Drucker, Mr. Murfree, Mr. Turlock, Malindy, the moonshiners, and the "desperate ladies" of Big Tree Junction all have stories waiting to be told about them. Pick one of the lesser characters from *Eight Mules to Monterey* and write a story in which this character is the central figure. You can tie your story to things that happened in Beatty's book, such as telling what happened to Joshua Drucker from his point of view, or you can make up your own plot about one of the characters.

Writer's Triangle © 1989

The Indian in the Cupboard

by Lynne Reid Banks
(Doubleday, 1985,
ISBN 0-385-17051-3;
in paperback,
Avon Camelot, 1982,
ISBN 0-380-60012-9).
Fantasy.

Summary: For his birthday, Omri gets a small plastic Indian from his friend Patrick, and a small, white metal cupboard from his brother Gillon. While Omri sleeps, the Indian who is in the cupboard comes to life. (Omri later discovers that anything plastic will come to life in the cupboard.) Quickly realizing that his Indian is not a plaything but a person, Omri makes friends with Little Bear and helps him establish a home in his room. Omri provides him with a horse, who gets scared and kicks Little Bear; a plastic medic from WWI to help with his injury; and a cowboy, who becomes his enemy. When Omri brings a plastic chief to life to provide Little Bear with company, the poor old man dies of a heart attack. Far from being unhappy, Little Bear is delighted and makes himself the chief. The big crisis of the book comes when Patrick "spills the beans" to the headmaster. At the end, Omri finds Little Bear a pretty plastic Indian wife, brings her to life, and then sends them back to their own time.

Comments: Highly entertaining, with outstanding character development for a light book. Imaginative as well as humorous, and plenty of dramatic tension. Although it is English, it is very familiar to U.S. students because of the cowboy and Indian theme.

Name _____ Room _____

The Indian in the Cupboard
by Lynne Reid Banks

**Meet with your discussion group before the book is
begun and talk about what you think it would be like
to have a miniature person you had to take care of.**

As you listen to the story, think about how Banks
makes her characters interesting by being so different
from one another. In particular,

▌ compare Omri's and Patrick's behaviors
▌ compare Little Bear's and Boone's behaviors

Schedule

Book Will Be Finished by _____

First Draft Due _____

Final Draft Due _____

Notes

_____

_____

_____

_____

_____

Writer's Triangle © 1989

The Indian in the Cupboard

by Lynne Reid Banks

Chapter 1

The first chapter is where authors introduce both the plot and the characters of a story. Now that you've heard the first chapter, discuss the following questions:

1. What significant things do you know about the main characters: Omri, Patrick, and the Indian?

Omri is a nice boy. He is happy with simple gifts, and he treats the Indian gently and with respect.

Patrick is selfish and perhaps a bit thoughtless. He gives Omri a gift he had no use for himself.

The Indian is courageous.

2. We also learn something about Omri's family. What are they like?

They are loving; his parents give him his dearest wish, a skateboard, and his brother Adiel gives him the helmet. Even his brother Gillon, who has no money, goes out to find something for him.

3. What is the plot or problem in this book going to be about?

Omri is going to have to deal with a live Indian who is only as large as his finger. He will have to feed him, care for him, hide him.

Chapter 2

In this chapter, in order to build reader interest, Lynne Reid Banks creates a crisis, an urgent problem. She also develops the fantasy of Little Bear by telling many details about him and showing the problems Omri has taking care of him.

1. What is the crisis? Is it a crisis for the reader or just for Omri?

Omri thinks he killed the Indian by leaving him shut up in the cupboard. It's a crisis only for Omri. We know he couldn't have killed him—there wouldn't be a story—but Omri is really scared.

2. **What things does Banks do to develop the fantasy? Think about all the things Omri has to do for Little Bear.**

Banks explores what someone with a tiny, live Indian would have to do to care for him. Basically, like anyone else, he needs food and shelter. For food, Omri provides corn, cheese, bread; for shelter, he gives him a blanket made of an old sweater and a teepee made of felt and sticks.

Chapter 3

This chapter deals with conflict. Conflict is when there are two things you want to do and you can't do both.

1. **What is Omri's conflict about the Indians?**

He is a little afraid of the Indian, who'd taken thirty scalps in the French and Indian War. Omri would like to share this whole awesome experience with adults, but he is afraid that if he does, they will take over and take the Indian and the cupboard away.

2. **Does Little Bear have a conflict about Omri?**

Somewhat, although he seems to be working it out. At first he was very afraid of Omri, even though he had no choice but to trust him. Now he seems to see him as a friendly spirit who obeys him and fulfills his wishes, especially when Omri gives him a horse.

Chapter 4

Banks makes her readers sensitive to the Indian's problems by having Omri become more aware of them. Chapter 4 says, "More and more, he found, he was able to see things from the Indian's point of view."

1. **What things does Omri visualize from the Indian's point of view when Little Bear is galloping around in the yard?**

He imagines they are in "wild, unbroken territory." Little stones become big boulders, weeds become trees, an ant is large enough to scare the horse, and bird's shadow is enormous and frightening.

2. **How does Omri's new way of seeing things help him solve the problem of Little Bear's leg injury?**

By seeing things from Little Bear's point of view, he knew he couldn't treat his injury; all his equipment would be too big. His thinking was becoming flexible, however, so when he noticed Tommy, the World War I medic, he realized the plastic medical equipment, turned real, could solve his problems.

Writer's Triangle © 1989

Chapter 5

1. Good authors make their characters distinctive. They give each character in the book a different personality and a unique way of speaking or behaving. How does the way Omri speaks differ from the way Tommy or Little Bear speak?

Omri speaks conventional English. Little Bear speaks broken English, omitting words such as *a, the*, and *is*. Tommy speaks with a lot of slang and language patterns associated with the British: "Right you are!" "Bit of a lark, this," "bloomin'," "rum dream," and so on.

2. Why does Banks have Little Bear build an Iroquois house?

Omri has already provided him with shelter, so it is mainly to provide interest. We enjoy thinking about what equipment he needs and watching how Omri figures out how to get it for him "in miniature." It also teaches us something about the Iroquois' lifestyle.

Chapter 6

1. When authors want to give their readers a lot of information, they must figure out a way to do it without being boring. What techniques does Banks use to teach us about the Iroquois Indians?

She has Omri go to the library to find out about Indians. In order to convey actual information without boring the reader, she reveals that Omri doesn't like to read, so she can have him dip into a book and read only those parts she wants to share with her reader. She also gives us information about building a longhouse by having Omri watch Little Bear build one.

2. Tension is building between Omri and Patrick over the "plastic" Indian. Banks is setting something up. What do you think will happen?

Answers will vary. They may include the idea that Patrick will find out about Little Bear or that he will ask questions and expose the presence of Little Bear. Some students may guess that Omri and Patrick are heading for a fight.

Chapter 7

1. How does Banks use Omri's brothers to create excitement in Chapter 7?

Omri thinks they've found Little Bear when they are in his room looking at the longhouse. This creates tension and reminds us how easily Omri's secret could be found out.

2. The events of Chapter 7 do a lot to reveal the differences between Omri and Patrick. What does Banks emphasize about Patrick's character in this chapter?

Once again, Patrick is revealed as thoughtless and selfish. We have already seen him give a useless gift to Omri. This time he is ready to bring a whole handful of soldiers to life without thinking about the consequences. Omri has to explain that when toys become real, they come with their own lives and ideas. Patrick is dissuaded only when he sees the dead Indian chief.

Chapter 8

1. How has Banks prepared us for the way Patrick behaves in this chapter?

Our previous encounters with Patrick show he is thoughtless and selfish. It is in character, then, for him to be determined to have a live person of his own and to treat his cowboy and horse carelessly once he has them. It is also in character for Patrick to demand that Omri bring the cowboy to school and to threaten Omri with exposure to get his own way.

2. A good author keeps bringing new problems into the story to keep us interested. What are the two new elements Banks brought into the story in Chapter 8 that make us want to read on?

Omri has to find a wife for Little Bear, and he has to cope with Patrick's cowboy and horse.

Chapter 9

1. Once again, Banks has created a completely new and interesting character in Boone. What characteristics does the cowboy have that make him memorable?

His speech patterns are "Texan cowboy" and very different from those of other characters in the book. He drinks a lot and sees things that aren't

Writer's Triangle © 1989

there. He tends to cry a lot, but he's no coward; in fact, he is always ready to fight. To add to the "fun," he doesn't like Indians.

2. **Each of the people brought to life so far has had a different explanation of who Omri is. What are these explanations and which do you think you'd be most likely to believe if you suddenly found yourself in the plastic people's situation?**

The Indian thinks he's some sort of magical spirit. The medic thought he was a dream, and the cowboy thinks he is a hallucination. Answers will vary, but most of us in that situation would probably think we were dreaming.

Chapter 10

What happens when Banks has Omri make Boone and Little Bear eat breakfast together? How does this make the story better?

A. We get to hear their prejudices and see them act out the hostilities of the cowboys and Indians of the American plains.

B. It forces Boone and Little Bear to deal with each other.

C. This adds interest and lets Banks show us more of the characters.

Chapter 11

The big worry about taking Boone and Little Bear to school is that someone will see them. This tension keeps us interested, turning pages to see if they get caught. What two major events in Chapter 11 keep the fear alive?

First, April sees Omri give Boone to Patrick and causes a small uproar among the children. Then, Little Bear stabs Omri several times with his knife. This causes Omri to cry out and call attention to himself in class and endanger his secret.

Chapter 12

Why do you think Patrick told Mr. Johnson about Little Bear?

Answers will vary, but may include the idea that he got flustered, or that the tension of the secret was so great, he "had to tell," thus relieving some of the tension.

Chapter 13

1. **What do you think would have happened if Mr. Johnson had believed his own eyes when Patrick showed him Little Bear?**

   He'd have probably confiscated him, called Patrick's parents, the press, scientists, and so on.

2. **Is it logical and realistic that Mr. Johnson doesn't believe what he saw and behaves the way he did?**

   Answers will vary, but should include that Mr. Johnson's reaction was a possible response.

3. **Banks has created many problems in this story—a lot of bad things have happened. She needs to turn the story back to being an entertaining adventure for Omri as well as for the reader. What two things does she include in Chapter 13 that accomplish this?**

   Omri has a wonderful time in his art class, and Patrick redeems himself in the toy shop, thus making him Omri's friend and part of the story again.

Chapter 14

1. **Losing the key would be a problem at any point in the story, but to increase our interest, Banks made it absolutely critical here. How did she make the lost key so important?**

   When Little Bear shoots Boone with his bow and arrow, they cannot get Tommy, the medic, to help treat him.

2. **How does Banks show that Little Bear is sorry he shot Boone?**

   He pulled the arrow out, he said he was sorry, he began to sob, he treated Boone, he stomped on his headdress, and he went off to his longhouse to be by himself.

Chapter 15

1. **What situations does Banks include that increase or help maintain suspense throughout Chapter 15? Think about what situations make you tense.**

   Omri wants to keep watch over Boone, and we are afraid that his mother or father might come in and catch him and Patrick with Little Bear and Boone. Another suspenseful element is Boone's physical condition. We don't know if he is going to survive. When we learn that Gillon's

Writer's Triangle © 1989

rat is loose somewhere in the house, probably under the floorboards in Omri's room, things get really tense. Finally, to heighten our fear of the rat, Banks has Little Bear go under the floorboards to look for the key. We can then worry that he will be attacked by the rat in a place where Omri and Patrick will be unable to help him. In short, Banks puts her characters in a series of increasingly dangerous situations.

2. Why do you think Banks has Little Bear find the key?

It's a way for him to make amends for shooting Boone, and it shows his courage.

3. How do you think Banks will end the story? Do you think Omri can keep Little Bear forever?

Answers will vary but should include some understanding of how difficult it would be to keep the little people indefinitely.

Chapter 16
Do you think Banks achieved a happy ending? Why or why not?

Answers may include:

A. Yes, because the little people were safe and got to go back to a place where they belonged. Omri still had the ability to bring them back if he wished, although we know this is not something he plans to do. The experience enriched his life, and the memories of Little Bear and Boone remain.

B. Not quite, because it is sad that Omri had to give up this magical household he had brought to life. He will miss Little Bear and Boone.

Writer's Triangle © 1989

Writing Activity

The Indian in the Cupboard
by Lynne Reid Banks

CHOOSE ONE WRITING ACTIVITY THAT INTERESTS YOU.

A. Pretend that you suddenly found yourself pulled into a little boy or girl's cupboard. Like Little Bear, you are much smaller than your owner. Write a story about your situation. Tell how you feel. What is your owner like? What does he or she do for you? What adventures do you have? How are your problems solved? How do you get back?

B. Some of Bank's humor comes when characters behave in inappropriate ways. For example, Little Bear has temper tantrums, most unusual in a proud Indian brave. Boone cries easily, which is unexpected in a tough cowboy. We laugh at personality twists like these.

Create a humorous animal character by having it behave in an uncharacteristic way. You might think about the traits we usually associate with certain animals: brave lion, timid mouse, sharp-eyed eagle, sly fox, slow sloth, playful puppy, or long-remembering elephant. Write a scene which shows your animal being an oddball.

Writer's Triangle © 1989

Night Journeys

by Avi
(Random House/
Pantheon, 1979,
ISBN 0-394-94116-0;
not available in
paperback).
Historical Fiction.

Summary: Peter York is overeager to track down two escaped indentured servants and angry that his Quaker guardian, who is the justice of the peace, is so negative about the hunt. The escapees turn out to be children, and when the girl looks as though she is going to get away, Peter shoots her. This is the turning point of the story. Tormented by guilt, Peter brings the girl food, promises to release the boy, who is in his woodshed, and finally decides to help them escape. In the end, he and his Quaker guardian reverse roles, and it is Peter who sets the moral example.

Comments: This book has action, drama, and significant moral issues to discuss. Interesting descriptions of life for poor farmers as well as for indentured servants make the book educational without being didactic.

Prelistening Focus

Night Journeys

by Avi

Meet with your discussion group before the book is begun and talk about whether it is ever right to break a law in order to help someone.

As you listen to the story, think about

▌ how the attitudes of the main characters change
▌ how people who are faced with moral dilemmas struggle to make good decisions

Schedule

Book Will Be Finished by _____

First Draft Due _____

Final Draft Due _____

Notes

_____

_____

_____

_____

_____

Writer's Triangle © 1989

Discussion Guide

Night Journeys

by Avi

Part One, Chapters 1-4

1. **Think about the words Avi uses to describe Mr. Shinn. What words or ideas does he include in his description that would make Mr. Shinn unappealing to a 12-year-old boy? (The discussion leader may want to reread the third and fourth paragraphs of Chapter 2 to help students recall Avi's words.)**

He says Mr. Shinn is heavy, ponderous, and slow. He rarely smiles, is generally silent, and seems devoid of emotion. He has pale features, grey hair, and imposing dignity. All this paints a picture of a somber, elderly man without much fun about him.

2. **Avi created a conflict between Mr. Shinn and Peter over Jumper, the horse. It's an interesting conflict because it has two arguable sides. What do you think? Was Mr. Shinn right to make Jumper part of the Shinn family possessions?**

Answers will vary. The argument for Mr. Shinn might be that he has made Peter a full part of his family. Peter shares whatever the Shinns have, and so he should do the same for them and share Jumper or whatever he has that they may need.

The argument for Peter's side is that he has lost everything except Jumper, and it is insensitive of Mr. Shinn to take his last possession from him, too.

3. **How does Avi show us that Mr. Shinn did not want to hunt the bondsmen down?**

Avi puts a rebuke in Mr. Shinn's voice when he says, "I presume there's a reward, or thee would not have come at such a time." When Peter picks up the gun, he speaks sharply, saying, "Bondsmen are not squirrels." He tells Peter he is obliged, implying he doesn't want to go, and says he will help only if he can do it lawfully without killing. We also see it from the attitude of the other men who want Mr. Shinn to watch at Morgan's Rock, the least likely spot for the bondsmen to cross. They don't say it, but it's clear that they are afraid if he were at a critical location, his lack of enthusiasm could ruin their chances at capturing the runaways.

Part One, Chapters 5-8

1. **Overly eager to capture the bondsmen and get the reward, Peter is contemptuous of Mr. Shinn for being slow and reluctant. Yet in comparing the two characters, Avi shows Mr. Shinn as more responsible and more effective than Peter. How do Peter's impatience and irritation with Mr. Shinn lead to the troubles he finds himself in at the end of this section?**

Peter is restless and goes off to explore the island, and then, afraid of being left, he runs too fast and falls, hurting his arm. Perhaps because of the pain in his arm, perhaps just because he was so distracted by the excitement of the impending hunt, he forgets his gun. He doesn't want to admit weakness or fault to Mr. Shinn, so he lies about how much his arm hurts, opening himself to further difficulty when he tries to pole himself across the river to go back for the gun.

2. **When Peter expresses disapproval of the bondsmen for breaking the law by trying to escape, Mr. Shinn tells him that "the law's a chain that keeps all as one. . . . But mind, it's still a chain." He is saying that the law restricts everyone's freedom, not just the felons'. How is Mr. Shinn's freedom restricted by the law?**

As justice of the peace, Mr. Shinn has to obey the law and track down the bondsmen, even though his sympathies are with the escapees, whom he doesn't want to catch.

3. *Hypocrite* **is a critical term for a person who believes one thing and acts another way. Peter thinks Mr. Shinn is a hypocrite because he doesn't want to catch the two bondsmen and yet goes on the hunt. Peter is also critical of him over the issue of oath taking (swearing to tell the truth or uphold the law). Mr. Shinn doesn't believe in it, so when his work as justice of the peace requires that he have someone take an oath, he has Mr. Dempsey do it for him. Although Peter is feeling very hostile toward Mr. Shinn, Avi presents Mr. Shinn in a more kindly light to the reader. We see him as a sincere, thoughtful, and careful man. Why do you think Avi has Peter see him in such a critical light?**

Avi needs to set up conflict in the book. To have adventures, Peter must be operating outside of Mr. Shinn's protection. If he is angry, resentful,

Writer's Triangle © 1989

or embarrassed in relation to his protector, it makes it reasonable for him to plan and act on his own.

Part Two, Chapters 1-3

Avi creates excitement in his book by letting his readers know or guess things before Peter does. His readers are then anxious about Peter's behavior, because they can see him making mistakes.

1. **What clues does Avi give us that Peter's plan for crossing the river is foolishly dangerous?**

   We know his arm is hurt, which made it hard for him to cross before. We know the current is very swift and strong. We also know that Peter is so filled with shame and so eager to prove himself that his judgment is cloudy. He really should go to Well's Falls and cross at the ferry.

2. **What clues does Avi give us to the identity of the girl?**

   Her clothes are ragged and too big for her. Her hair is unkempt. She is weak, thin, and undersized, suggesting poor care and nourishment. There is fear and hardness in her face. She clenches her fist as though there were something wrong with her hand and speaks in a suspicious tone. A nonswimmer, she is willing to risk her life crossing the river, and she is nervous when Peter mentions the bondsmen.

Part Two, Chapters 4-6

1. **After initial fear of him, the girl seems to put her trust in Peter and does whatever he tells her to do. What effect does this have on Peter?**

   He begins to feel good again, his ego restored by her trust. Possibly her faith in him gives him a false sense of power and, coupled with his eagerness to regain the gun, pushes him to try something he would not otherwise try: taking a nonswimmer across a dangerous river. Her trust also makes him responsible for her, and when they do get into trouble, he tries to protect her.

2. **Now that Peter knows the girl is one of the bondsmen, what do you think he is going to do?**

   Answers will vary. Some students may think the bond they developed in the struggle to survive the river and the protective role he has assumed will make him decide to help her. Others may think he will keep his eye on the reward and glory that would come to him if he captured her.

3. Who do you think the other bondsman might be?

Answers will vary. Students should be aware, however, that the other bondsman probably does not fit Peter's initial vision of a cutpurse, scamp, or rogue, either. More likely it is another sympathetic character.

Part Three, Chapters 1-3

1. What clues has Avi given us to help us understand why the girl ran off and hid from Peter?

We know that Peter alerted her to his interest in the bondsmen when he told her he was part of the hunting party, so we expect that she will realize he is a danger to her as soon as he has seen her hand. We know from her initial behavior with Peter that she is wary and suspicious, so we should not be surprised that she is not fooled by his pretense of ignorance in an attempt to lure her to Mistress Shinn.

2. Peter is basically a decent person. How does Avi make it believable that he would shoot the girl?

Avi has Peter develop a fantasy in which he is the triumphant captor of the girl. This fantasy is shattered when the girl runs away from him. Peter's reaction is anger. He feels that she betrayed him by not waiting around for him to haul her in. He becomes more and more frantic as he searches for her, so when he finally sees her, he is intent on catching her at all cost.

3. Why does Avi have Peter throw away the gun?

This action clearly shows his readers that they are at the turning point of the story. Appalled by his behavior, Peter is no longer the hunter, no longer interested in capturing the girl. All he wants now is to atone for what he has done.

Part Three, Chapters 4-6

1. How does Avi show us that the Shinns care about Peter?

In Chapter 3, Mr. Shinn comes looking for him, gives Peter his own jacket, and puts the young man near him on Jumper even though he is wet. In this section, Mistress Shinn is alarmed at the sight of him and wants to help. All she can do is give him a lot of food, which she does. The family holds a prayer meeting where Mr. Shinn talks of Peter's near escape. Mr. Shinn forgives him his work the next day and repays the man whose boat Peter ruined. Although the gun was a valuable, not-

Writer's Triangle © 1989

easily-replaced piece of equipment, Mr. Shinn does not scold him about losing it.

2. **How does Avi make us sympathetic to Elizabeth even though she admits she stole the ring?**

He makes her young and vulnerable. He gives her a good reason for stealing: she was hungry and that was the only way she could get anything to eat. He puts her with Mr. Tolivar, a harsh master who obviously does not treat her well and makes her punishment very severe: she will be bonded until she comes of age.

3. **Peter is uneasy, afraid that Mr. Shinn knows what he is about, even though he has not challenged him directly. What mistakes did Avi have Peter make that might cause Mr. Shinn to suspect that Peter knows where Elizabeth is?**

Peter's explanation of how he lost the gun was confused. Mr. Shinn heard the gunshot when Peter shot Elizabeth, but Peter claimed he'd already lost the gun. Peter asked how old the prisoner was, a clue that he might know the other one was young. Peter took a lot of food for lunch and brought it outside, which was unusual behavior.

Part Four, Chapters 1-3

1. **Why is Peter still angry with Mr. Shinn even after he revealed that he planned to ask Mr. Tolivar to free the boy?**

He thinks Mr. Shinn should free the boy, not ask Mr. Tolivar to do so. He is also angry that Mr. Shinn is pushing him to go on the search party or to speculate where the girl might be hiding.

2. **Why does Avi make Mr. Shinn so eager for Peter to go on the search party?**

By doing so, Avi sets up a puzzle for the reader. We know Mr. Shinn has cause to suspect that Peter might know where Elizabeth is hiding, but we don't know how he feels about the search. On the one hand, he has said that he lacks the stomach for the hunt, in which case he might want Peter to lead the party in a direction away from the girl. On the other hand, he is a strong believer in upholding the law, and it is his job to bring the runaways back. If this is his position, then he would be very angry at Peter for undermining the search effort. The uncertainty adds tension to the story and makes us unsure of the outcome.

3. **In what other ways does Avi make this part of the book tense and exciting so that the reader will be anxious to read the last part to find out what happens?**

Writer's Triangle © 1989

He has his characters operating in the dark, making it possible for them to get lost or hurt. He has the search party still out looking for the girl, which greatly increases their chances of getting caught. He has Peter determine that he will have no choice but to run away without knowing if the other two will welcome him.

Part Four, Chapters 4-6

1. Why does Peter, the moment the two children have their freedom, decide that he does not want to go with them?

As soon as Mr. Shinn lets him free the runaways, it removes the barrier that had grown between them. His main reason for running was not so much to avoid punishment, but to avoid the humiliation of being thrown out by Mr. Shinn. He now knows that Mr. Shinn is on his side, and he is prepared to return to the family that has taken him in and made him one of them.

2. What does Avi show us when he has Peter give Elizabeth and Robert his horse?

We now know that Peter feels secure. In the beginning of the book, he was possessive about Jumper because he had nothing else. Now that he has a family again, he doesn't mind giving Jumper away. Of course, by doing so he can make final restitution to Elizabeth for the injury he caused her, showing us the depth of his remorse and the strength of his character.

3. During the course of the book, Peter's attitude and behavior regarding the bondsmen changes radically. How did Peter's changed attitude and behavior influence Mr. Shinn?

Mr. Shinn was never eager to hunt the bondsmen, but he believed it important to do his duty and uphold the law. His distaste for the job makes him something of a fence-sitter, however. When he goes on the hunt, he hopes the bondsmen won't come. When he realizes that Peter knows something about the runaways, he hopes Peter will take the responsibility for freeing them. At the end of the book, he admits to Peter that Peter was right and thanks him for acting for him. Peter's courage and determination to do what he thought was right, even if it meant breaking the law and being punished, set an example for Mr. Shinn.

Writer's Triangle © 1989

Writing Activity

Night Journeys
by Avi

CHOOSE ONE WRITING ACTIVITY THAT INTERESTS YOU.

A. Peter and Mr. Shinn both came to the conclusion that the law about returning bondsmen was wrong. They decided that it was more moral to break the law than to follow it. We have had to face a similar ethical problem in our own time. Civil rights leaders looked at laws that made black people second-class citizens and said those laws were wrong. For example, when Rosa Parks, a gentle black seamstress, refused to give up her bus seat to a white person, she was arrested. People rallied behind her, and the ministers of Montgomery, Alabama, including Martin Luther King, Jr., organized a bus boycott. Write a scene in which a 1955 family who was on that bus discusses the incident at dinner. Let family members express and defend different points of view. Have your family reach an agreement just the way Mr. Shinn and Peter did.

B. Avi wanted to make Mr. Shinn redeem himself with Peter and the reader. The way he does this is to have Mr. Shinn reverse his position on returning the bondsmen and then apologize to Peter for not setting a good example. Show that you understand this technique by choosing a villain from a familiar folk tale (for example, the wolf from *The Three Little Pigs,* the witch stepmother from *Snow White,* the stepsisters from *Cinderella*). Rewrite the ending of the folk tale you chose. Have the villain redeem himself or herself by behaving as Mr. Shinn did—by showing a change of heart, apologizing, and expressing a plan to behave better in the future. Don't make this a single speech. Be sure your characters act naturally and have a conversation about the situation. Have your characters move around, respond to what each other says, and show their feelings.

Sarah Bishop

by Scott O'Dell
(Houghton Mifflin, 1980,
ISBN 0-395-29185-2;
in paperback,
Scholastic, 1982,
ISBN 0-590-32120-X).
Historical Fiction.

Summary: Sarah Bishop is a 15-year-old girl caught between the forces of the Patriots and the Tories at the outbreak of the Revolutionary War. Her father, who sympathizes with the British, is tarred and feathered and his home and farm are burned. When he dies, Sarah is homeless, so she goes to work for a local innkeeper. When Sarah goes in search of her brother, Chad, who had joined the Revolutionary Army, she is accused by a British officer of starting a fire and is arrested. She escapes, but this puts her on the run. She hides out in a cave near Long Pond and, with the help of an Indian family, survives the winter. The villain in this book of multiple villains is a purple-nosed hunter, Sam Goshen. He tries to molest her after giving her a ride and then turns up again when she is living in the cave. This time he is hurt, and Sarah must take him in. When she seems almost ready to trust people again, a Quaker shopkeeper accuses her of witchcraft. She survives the accusation and makes friends with the shopkeeper's son.

Comments: A serious book for older students, *Sarah Bishop* takes a look at the less glamorous side of the American Revolution. The harshness of the people's lives and the cruelty of the ignorant and the powerful are examined without whitewash. It makes for heavy reading. It is, however, beautifully written and might be a good foil to a book such as *Johnny Tremain*.

Writer's Triangle © 1989

Prelistening Focus

Sarah Bishop
by Scott O'Dell

Meet with your discussion group before the book is begun and talk about what it might have been like to have been the child of a Tory during the American Revolution.

As you listen to the story, think about

▮ the things Scott O'Dell does to present a fair picture of both sides of the Revolutionary War

▮ the way O'Dell includes facts about the customs of the eighteenth century to make his story come alive

Schedule

Book Will Be Finished by _____

First Draft Due _____

Final Draft Due _____

Notes

_____

_____

_____

_____

_____

Sarah Bishop

by Scott O'Dell

Chapters 1 and 2

After listening to these two chapters, you know that O'Dell has set the stage for trouble. How does he build suspense?

O'Dell builds suspense by including several threatening incidents. There is gunfire aimed toward the Bishop house, friction over which side to support in the American Revolution, a gang of young men who burn Tory property, machinery in Purdy's mill that stops at midnight, and discussion of witches. The greatest suspense, however, comes because Mr. Bishop faces danger. He's bitter about the rebellion and believes he should stand up for what he thinks. Mr. Purdy tells Sarah that she doesn't need much grist since her father's a Tory who talks too much and won't be around much longer.

Chapters 3 and 4

An author of a historical fiction book must give a lot of information to the reader. O'Dell gets some of the Patriot positions across efficiently by putting a Tory and a Patriot in a single family and having them confront each other. What historical information did you learn about the Revolution in these two chapters?

In these times of trouble, people like Mr. Bishop put their money into silverware and buried it for safekeeping. Thomas Paine's pamphlet, *Common Sense,* inspired many Americans to revolt against King George, against tyranny. Young men like Chad and David often had an unrealistic picture of what war was like when they enlisted. They thought it would be short and that they'd have plenty to eat. Mr. Bishop tells them they'll walk more than ride, be cold and hungry, and will have to face the fierce Hessian professional soldiers. Patriot soldiers went to war poorly prepared. For example, Chad Bishop goes off to fight without a gun.

Chapters 5, 6, 7, and 8

Going beyond the usual issues of freedom and justice, O'Dell forces us to examine the behavior of people in trying times. How does this

Writer's Triangle © 1989

technique change our perceptions about the American Revolution?

Answers will vary but may include the idea that O'Dell shows us Patriots were not all educated and fair people. Some were hostile and cruel. In a war where liberty and fairness were critical issues, Patriots tried and punished Mr. Bishop without a fair hearing.

Chapter 9 and 10

1. **What do you think O'Dell wanted us to think about when he named the tavern Sarah worked in The Lion and the Lamb?**

It's a way of getting the reader to think about the strong living in peace with the weak, a counterpoint to the violence of war. Since the lion is a symbol of England, it shows England living in peace with America, the weak lamb.

2. **To make us a part of the historical scene, an author must give us many authentic details. What do we learn about these times from Sarah's experiences at the tavern?**

The tavern was neutral ground frequented by soldiers from both sides, depending on which side was in control of the area. It was a good place to gather news, and Sarah tried to learn where Chad might be. Most of the American officers and soldiers who visited did not want peace; they wanted to kill every British soldier but never seemed to think that they might be killed. Only British officers visited, because the British army forbade officers and soldiers to mix socially. Although the British officers were polite, the Hessians were fierce and bragged about taking no prisoners. Local farmers were eager to sell their produce before soldiers raided their farms. Sarah learned how to powder the British officers' wigs. When one of these officers gave her a note to the captain in charge of all rebel prisoners to help her try to find out if Chad was a prisoner, we can see the friendliness between the British and civilian Americans.

Chapters 11, 12, and 13

Just in case the tarring and feathering of Mr. Bishop has shifted our sympathies too far to the Tory side, O'Dell introduces Captain Cunningham. How is Cunningham's behavior similar to that of the Patriots who tarred and feathered Mr. Bishop, and what effect does his behavior have on the reader?

A. Like the Patriots who tarred and feathered Mr. Bishop, Captain

Writer's Triangle © 1989

Cunningham is cruel and intolerant. He is power-hungry and does not give Sarah a fair hearing.

B. Because neither side is totally honorable and neither side considers the effect of its behavior on innocent people such as young Sarah, we become more objective readers and look at all sides of the issue.

Chapters 14, 15, and 16

O'Dell shows us the depth of Sarah's despair and anger through her behavior in regard to the Bible. What has made her bitter and what does she do to show it?

Sarah is bitter because her father and her brother have died and because she has been treated unfairly by Captain Cunningham. As a result, she rejects her father's faith and teachings, especially the passage in Matthew about "loving your enemies." She tears that page from the Bible and burns it.

Chapters 17, 18, 19, and 20

Sarah decides to cope with danger by running away. How does O'Dell make it believable that Sarah will escape and survive?

A. Sarah is strong and independent and she gets what she needs, even if she must sacrifice something special.

B. She sells her long blond hair to a wig shop for money to buy supplies.

C. The ferryman sells her a musket and teaches her how to use it.

D. She outsmarts Sam Goshen and escapes to Ridgeford on his horse.

Chapters 21, 22, and 23

1. **What skills does O'Dell give Sarah that enable her to survive in the wilderness?**

O'Dell gave Sarah knowledge of the wilderness and a practical mind. She knew how to make the cave habitable, thus coping with her need for shelter. She blocked the mouth of the cave so that the bats could not fly back in, and she cleared the heavy air in the cave with a pine fire. She built a lean-to as well as a birch-bark door. O'Dell also made it clear that she could supply herself with food. She caught fish and killed deer and geese. She gathered acorns, pounded them into flour, and stored the flour in gourd containers. She knew how to use goose feathers to make warm comforters, prepare a deer hide, make rush lights, and form candles from gourds, deer tallow, and blanket threads.

Writer's Triangle © 1989

2. **Why does O'Dell include the white bat?**

It shows Sarah making a connection with another living thing. She's rejected people and God, but this is a first step back.

Chapters 24, 25, and 26

It's important for authors to vary the pace of their story. When tense periods alternate with periods of calm, authors can better capture their audience. O'Dell uses this technique in this section. Which parts are calm and which parts are tense?

O'Dell first sets up a brief, tense skirmish with a hostile Indian who claims to own the entire area. Sarah refuses to be driven off and scares the Indian away with her musket. In contrast, O'Dell shows Sarah playing a light-hearted game with the white bat and naming him Gabriel for the Angel Gabriel. Continuing in this peaceful vein, the friendly Longknife family arrives and helps Sarah prepare for winter. O'Dell shows that war and terror have begun to fade.

Chapters 27, 28, and 29

In what ways has Sarah changed since she tore out the Bible page about "loving your enemies"?

Sarah is less angry, less insistent about being away from everybody, and more willing to show compassion towards an enemy—Sam Goshen.

Chapters 30 and 31

1. **What things does Sarah do in dealing with Sam Goshen that make him hate her?**

Sarah throws his crutch in the fire and reads him threatening Bible stories. She fixes Sam's gun so he can't fire it, locks him out of the cave and threatens to shoot at him through the door.

2. **O'Dell is laying the groundwork for the next meeting between Sarah and Sam. What do you think might happen when Sarah and Sam Goshen meet again?**

Answers will vary but should include the strong possibility of friction and vindictiveness.

Chapters 32 and 33

Good authors often set up parallel experiences to intensify meaning. How was Sarah's experience in the wilderness similar to the experience of her muskrat?

Like the muskrat, Sarah needed this time of healing. She lives alone, healing her spirit, developing self-reliance and courage in preparation for facing her own kind.

Chapters 34 and 35

Why do you think O'Dell put the snake in the story?

The snake

A. adds interest and excitement,

B. is an unexpected enemy and alerts the reader to the presence of danger in unexpected places,

C. is traditionally a symbol of evil, and

D. provides O'Dell with a chance to show us how Sarah handles this enemy.

Chapters 36, 37, and 38

Just the way the snake popped up unexpectedly, a human danger pops up unexpectedly in Ridgeford. How does the way Sarah handles the danger caused by the accusation of witchcraft show her maturity and character development?

Sarah is not going to be intimidated. She ran away when she was accused by Captain Cunningham, but she refuses to run away from these accusers. It shows she has finished running from her problems.

Chapters 39, 40, and 41

1. **O'Dell has used the snake as a symbol that stands for Sarah's enemies. How does Sarah's decision not to shoot the copperhead reflect her return to her father's teachings?**

Sarah has decided to forgive her enemy, even though, as her father says, "it's difficult."

2. **How do you think Isaac might have influenced her behavior?**

Isaac showed her love and talked to her about the importance of love. He used Matthew's words in the Bible to help save her from the witch hunters.

Writer's Triangle © 1989

Sarah Bishop

by Scott O'Dell

CHOOSE ONE WRITING ACTIVITY THAT INTERESTS YOU.

A. At every significant point in the plot of a story, an author makes decisions that affect the direction and outcome of the book. In *Sarah Bishop,* O'Dell chooses to make her an orphan and to have her brother die, leaving her completely alone. He chooses to have her threatened by Captain Cunningham. He chooses to have her encounter Sam Goshen, a dishonorable, unpleasant man. He could have had her meet a helpful person. He chooses to have Mr. Morton and other men from the town of Ridgeford become her enemies instead of her friends.

Suppose he had made a different choice in any of these places. Suppose her brother had turned out to be alive. Suppose Captain Cunningham had not accused her of setting the fire. Suppose, instead of Sam, she had met another girl in circumstances like her own. Suppose Mr. Morton was friendly. Rewrite one scene from the book, showing the change you have chosen, and indicate how this change might affect the direction or outcome of the book.

B. In Chapters 3 and 4, O'Dell gives us a lot of information about the issues of the American Revolution by putting a Tory and a Patriot in the same family and having them confront each other. Show your understanding of this technique by setting a story at the time of the Civil War. Put a Union sympathizer in a Confederate household. Write a scene in which the Union sympathizer has a fight with his or her family. In the course of confrontation, include all the information you want to give your readers about the issues of the war. You may have to do some research about the Civil War to make your scene vivid and accurate.

NOVELS FOR INDEPENDENT READING

- ▼ The Dark Is Rising
- ▼ The 18th Emergency
- ▼ The Great Gilly Hopkins
- ▼ Hazel Rye
- ▼ Ida Early Comes Over the Mountain
- ▼ One-eyed Cat
- ▼ One More Flight
- ▼ The Sign of the Beaver
- ▼ This Time of Darkness
- ▼ Tuck Everlasting
- ▼ The White Mountains
- ▼ Words by Heart
- ▼ A Wrinkle in Time

The Dark Is Rising

by Susan Cooper (Macmillan/Margaret K. McElderry, 1973, ISBN 0-689-30317-3; in paperback, Macmillan/Aladdin,1976, ISBN 0-689-70420-8, and Collier Macmillan, 1986, ISBN 0-689-71087-9). Fantasy.

Listening cassette (Cat. #394-76904-X) is available from Random House Media, Dept. 437, 400 Hahn Road, Westminster, MD 21157-9939.

Summary: For eleven years, Will Stanton has lived as an ordinary boy, but on Midwinter's Eve, the night before his birthday, strange things happen as the forces of evil begin to rise. Will learns that he is one of the Old Ones, immortals destined to keep the world from domination by the Dark. His role is that of the sign seeker, and throughout the twelve days of Christmas, as he fulfills his destiny of finding the six magical signs, he is drawn into a mystical and dramatic battle of epic proportions.

Comments: A brilliant, exciting book, *The Dark Is Rising* sweeps back and forth in time and in and out of our present mundane world into a world torn by cosmic forces. It carries the reader on wonderful leaps of imagination. For poor readers who may have difficulty with the literary style, the tape recording of the story helps.

Name _____   Room _____

The Dark Is Rising
by Susan Cooper

Meet with your discussion group before you begin reading and talk about how you would feel if you were told that you were not a regular kid but someone who had strange and wondrous powers that would help save the world from evil.

The Dark Is Rising is a fantasy. As you read it, think about

▮ how Susan Cooper makes it believable that an 11-year-old boy is destined to be a key player in defeating the forces of evil in the world

▮ how an ominous (fearful) mood is created and maintained throughout the book

Schedule

Fact Check Test _____

Discussion _____

First Draft Due _____

Final Draft Due _____

Notes

_____

_____

_____

_____

_____

Name _____   Room _____

The Dark Is Rising
by Susan Cooper

1. What color was the horse that Will got to ride?

_____

2. Where was Will supposed to put all his signs?

_____

3. Who waited for Will in the great hall behind the huge carved doors that sat alone and tall on the white slope?

_____

4. The wooden sign had to be renewed every hundred years. What was used to help renew this sign?

_____

5. Where was the Book of Gramarye hidden?

_____

6. What had to happen before the Rider was able to enter Will's house on Christmas Eve?

_____

7. Where did Will get the mask that the Hunter wore in the battle against the Dark?

_____

8. Who called the forces of the Dark into the Manor on the night of the snowstorm?

_____

9. Which member of Will's family did the Rider put in a spell during the rainstorm?

_____

10. What sign did Will take from the hands of the dead king on the ship?

_____

The Dark Is Rising
by Susan Cooper

1. What color was the horse that Will got to ride?

   white

2. Where was Will supposed to put all his signs?

   on his belt

3. Who waited for Will in the great hall behind the huge carved doors that sat alone and tall on the white slope?

   Merriman and the Lady, or the Old Ones

4. The wooden sign had to be renewed every hundred years. What was used to help renew this sign?

   fire

5. Where was the Book of Gramarye hidden?

   in the clock

6. What had to happen before the Rider was able to enter Will's house on Christmas Eve?

   Will's father invited him in, or he had to be invited in.

7. Where did Will get the mask that the Hunter wore in the battle against the dark?

   His brother sent it to him for his birthday and Christmas.

8. Who called the forces of the Dark into the Manor on the night of the snowstorm?

   the Walker

9. Which member of Will's family did the Rider put in a spell during the rainstorm?

   Mary, or his sister

10. What sign did Will take from the hands of the dead king on the ship?

    water

The Dark Is Rising
by Susan Cooper

Mood

1. Cooper sets the mood of her book in the first chapter. What hints does she give us in the first chapter that something strange is going on?

Animals are afraid of Will; rocks behave strangely; the tramp is called "the Walker" by Mr. Dawson—an odd name; Mr. Dawson warns that "tomorrow will be bad beyond imagining"; the impending storm is frightening; Will gets the Sign; the radio screeches when he comes near; fear grips him in bed; the skylight collapses with snow, and the rook feather is there, too.

2. Cooper has Will discover his powers gradually. Why doesn't she have someone such as Merriman tell him immediately what he can do?

It would destroy the mystery and suspense; it would keep us from identifying the normal boy in him.

Setting

1. Where does Will live when the story opens?

Huntercombe, England, which is in Buckinghamshire.

2. What is the setting of the story when Will is transported?

Same place but years earlier.

3. Why is it effective for Cooper to have parts of the story happen in Old, Old Times?

This makes it mysterious. We accept magical things happening in past times that would be hard to accept in a modern setting. When these things weave in and out of the present, it makes us feel the continuous presence of evil (the Dark). The Dark stretches over centuries, reaching from old times to now.

CONFLICT/PLOT

1. In a fantasy like *The Dark Is Rising,* the conflict is often a battle between the forces of good and evil. Who represents the forces of good in this book, and who represents evil?

Old Ones such as Merriman, the Old Lady, Mr. Dawson, and Will fight for good, and the Rider and Maggie represent evil.

2. Why does Cooper have the Old Ones fight the Rider and battle cold and howling noises, rather than go to battle with someone super-evil, such as Hitler? Why is her way more powerful?

Her way is symbolic. Any single mortal (person) comes and goes, but evil stays. Hitler died, but all evil didn't die with him. When Cooper's forces fight each other, it is for control, not death.

CHARACTER

1. How does Cooper let us know that the Rider is evil?

His towering size, his blazing eyes, and looming presence are frightening: He tears wolfishly at his bread, rides a huge, midnight stallion, and becomes furious when the smith pulls Will out of his way. Moreover, Will's senses tell him something's wrong. When Will sees him, the brightness leaves the sky, and he knows he must not break bread with him. Cooper also sets up a contrast to the white mare, who is gentle and is shod with the symbol of the forces of Light.

2. At one time the Walker served the forces of Light. Why did he switch?

He didn't like the way Merriman treated him. Despite all his devotion, he was made to risk his life, and he realized that Merriman was ready to let him die if it would serve the forces of Light. This made him feel uncared for and so he was vulnerable to an offer from the Dark.

Do real people who are good ever get tempted to do bad things?

Answers will vary.

Who might Cooper want the Walker to represent or symbolize?

Man, or all of us.

3. It was no accident that Will, an 11-year-old boy, turned out to be the hero of Cooper's dramatic fight between good and evil. Why was he a good choice?

It's fun to identify with someone like ourselves who has something wonderful happen to him. He is so ordinary at first that we identify with him and believe he really exists or could exist.

SIGNIFICANCE

1. Why do you think Cooper wants us to think about the forces of Light and Dark?

She wants us to think about how there is evil in the world and ways in which people might combat it.

2. Suppose you discovered that you were destined to be an Old One. What evil might you have to fight in today's world?

Answers will vary.

SIGNS

Why do you think Cooper chose the Signs she did? That is, iron, bronze, wood, stone, fire, and water.

Fire and water represent power. Iron, stone, and bronze represent the ages of man and are powerful in themselves. Wood is a living thing that must be renewed.

The Dark Is Rising
by Susan Cooper

CHOOSE ONE WRITING ACTIVITY THAT INTERESTS YOU.

A. To create a sense of mystery, you do not have to have old castles, ghosts, or graveyard settings. A funny look on someone's face, an unexpected happening, or a sense that something (you don't know what) is about to happen can be even more effective. Look at the first chapter of *The Dark Is Rising* again to see how Cooper makes extraordinary events happen in a familiar, ordinary setting. Examples are animals being restless, the radio screeching, and the skylight collapsing with snow.

   Create an opening scene for a mystery story. Make unusual things happen in an ordinary setting. You can use weather, peoples' behavior, or fear of something to set the scene. Intensify your mood by using suspenseful language, such as "an eerie shadow in the baby's nursery," "a twisted smile on the doctor's face," or "a disquieting silence."

B. In a fantasy, the author creates a world in which magic is possible. In *The Dark Is Rising* time travel occurs and people and objects possess strange powers.

   You are going to write a fantasy. Think of something that you can turn into a magic object. Write a scene in which you describe the object and show its fantastic powers at work.

The 18th Emergency

by Betsy Byars
(Viking, 1973,
ISBN 0-670-29055-6;
in paperback,
Penguin/Puffin, 1981,
ISBN 0-14-031451-2).
Realistic
Fiction/Humor.

Summary: When Marv Hammerman catches Benjie writing Marv's name on the chart near the Neanderthal man, Benjie's life becomes one of terror. There is no question about it, Marv is going to get him. Benjie—or Mouse, as his friends call him—worries about it, sneaks around, and tries to remember his friend Ezzie's solutions for surviving 17 emergencies, which he had gleaned from comic books and movies. At the end, Mouse realizes that he has injured Marv's honor and he must give Marv a chance to reclaim it. Mouse goes to find him, takes his beating, and earns some self-respect and the respect of friends. Ezzie even calls him Benjie now instead of Mouse.

Comments: Written with a great deal of humor, this story appeals strongly. The book is simply written and short. Because it has a single-strand plot and a realistic, satisfying resolution, it works well with less sophisticated readers.

Prereading Focus

The 18th Emergency
by Betsy Byars

Meet with your discussion group before you begin reading and talk about how you would feel and what you would do if the biggest, meanest, toughest kid in school was after you.

As you read, think about

▮ what it's like to face up to fear and terror
▮ how Byars achieved suspense with humor
▮ what honor can be

Marv Hammerman

Schedule

Fact Check Test _____

Discussion _____

First Draft Due _____

Final Draft Due _____

Notes

_____

_____

_____

_____

_____

Name _____ Room _____

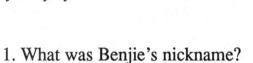

Fact Check Test

The 18th Emergency
by Betsy Byars

1. What was Benjie's nickname?

_____

2. Why was Benjie's father out of town so much?

_____

3. Ezzie made a list of threatening situations and how to survive them. What did he and Benjie call these situations?

_____

4. What did Benjie write next to the picture of the Neanderthal man?

_____

5. Where did Benjie try to put Viola Angotti?

_____

6. What did Benjie draw next to the names and labels he put on everything?

_____

7. What unexpected, weird green thing did the boys pull out of Garbage Dog's mouth?

_____

8. What color sweat shirt did Hammerman's buddy always wear?

_____

9. What game did Benjie play with Mr. Casino?

_____

10. What did the lady from the lower apartment do for Benjie at the end of the book?

_____

The 18th Emergency

by Betsy Byars

1. What was Benjie's nickname?

Mouse

2. Why was Benjie's father out of town so much?

He was a trucker.

3. Ezzie made a list of threatening situations and how to survive them. What did he and Benjie call these situations?

emergency, or emergencies

4. What did Benjie write next to the picture of the Neanderthal man?

Marv Hammerman

5. Where did Benjie try to put Viola Angotti?

a garbage can

6. What did Benjie draw next to the names and labels he put on everything?

arrows

7. What unexpected, weird green thing did the boys pull out of Garbage Dog's mouth?

turtle

8. What color sweat shirt did Hammerman's buddy always wear?

black

9. What game did Benjie play with Mr. Casino?

checkers

10. What did the lady from the lower apartment do for Benjie at the end of the book?

She cleaned him up after the fight.

Writer's Triangle © 1989

The 18th Emergency
by Betsy Byars

Plot

1. What causes the conflict in *The 18th Emergency*?

Benjie (Mouse) labels Marv a Neanderthal man, and Marv wants revenge.

2. Betsy Byars uses suspense and humor to keep us involved and interested in what is basically a simple plot. Identify suspenseful and humorous incidents and techniques that kept you interested.

Suspense:

▮ The main suspenseful element is that until the end of the book, she makes a mystery of the way Benjie and Marv will resolve their conflict.

▮ Through a series of near misses, partly arranged by Benjie, the boys don't encounter each other, but the threat is always there.

▮ Byars does not immediately share with the reader that Benjie decides to find Marv Hammerman. We know only that he has a plan that is so scary it could turn him into a scared, curled shrimp.

▮ At the end Byars uses a device of a time countdown to heighten suspense. Benjie notes the time, minute by minute, as he searches for Marv.

Humor:

▮ The boys' names, Mouse and Hammerman, are descriptive.

▮ Benjie's tendency to dramatize and exaggerate his situation makes the tone of the book humorous rather than serious.

▮ The emergencies that Ezzie and Benjie talk about are outrageous, and their solutions are generally impossible.

- Benjie's labels and arrows are clever.

- Benjie can laugh at himself. The story he tells about how Viola Angotti refused to be thrown in a school trash can shows that he's not afraid to tell a story in which he comes out looking weak and silly.

- Garbage Dog with his short feet and large appetite adds a light touch.

3. Good authors sometimes employ a technique called a plot twist, which is a part in the story where the plot suddenly goes in a completely unexpected direction. What is the plot twist in *The 18th Emergency*?

Benjie's decision to find Marv Hammerman and take his beating.

4. Everybody's family is different. In every family there are problems and tensions. Byars deliberately created tensions in Benjie's family situation so that it would contribute to the plot. What factors in Benjie's family situation create tensions?

His mother is busy and doesn't take him seriously. Perhaps this is because he tends to get dramatic and cry wolf too often. Perhaps she is just not as sensitive to him as she ought to be. Mrs. Casino, for example, compliments him loudly to his mother, but his mother only responds with extra instructions. His father is on the road and so is not there to give Benjie support either. All this isolates Benjie and throws him on his own. He has to solve his problem himself.

CHARACTER

1. Why did Benjie write "Marv Hammerman" and draw an arrow next to the picture of the Neanderthal man on the school chart?

Although Benjie said he didn't know why, we could guess that he had gotten into the habit of making these little labels on things and did it without a whole lot of thought. We could also guess that at the moment tiny Benjie wrote this, he felt a sense of power over the hulking, slow-witted Marv. Other possible reasons include Benjie's exercise of his creative imagination and desire for attention. Of course, he gets more attention than he expected.

2. Without telling us many details about her characters, Byars nonetheless creates for each character a sharp image in our minds. Think how she does this by comparing and contrasting the characteristics of Benjie and Marv. How are they alike and how are they different?

They are alike in that they are two boys from the same neighborhood in the same grade. Both boys want respect from their peers, and both boys

Writer's Triangle © 1989

have problems with this. Their differences are that Marv is dull—he's been left back so much that he's bigger than other sixth graders—while Benjie is small but bright and imaginative. Marv tries to gain respect by scaring smaller children; Benjie tries to fit in by being funny and kind, for example, by helping Garbage Dog and Mr. Casino.

3. What do you think it would be like to be Marv Hammerman?

He is bigger and stronger than everyone in the sixth grade, but he's been left back a couple of times and looks like a "Neanderthal man." This must make him feel pretty inadequate sometimes, and he possibly acts tough to compensate. We get the clue to this when Benjie remembers how vulnerable Marv looked when Benjie labeled him a "Neanderthal man."

4. Why did Byars include Mr. Casino in the story? Does he shed light on other characters? Does his presence affect the plot?

Benjie's kindness to him shows Benjie as both kind and responsible. The plot becomes tense when Benjie thinks Marv will get him because he is saddled with Mr. Casino.

SETTING

1. In what kind of a neighborhood did Byars choose to set the story?

It's a working-class, city neighborhood.

2. What details does Byars give us about Benjie's neighborhood that make it easy for us to visualize it?

Apartment houses are run-down, garbage is on the street, kids tend to fight a lot—there is a clue to this when the woman cleans him up—not much adult supervision, no Little League, piano lessons, and so on.

THEME

A theme of a book is an idea or concept that the author explores. In *The 18th Emergency,* the theme is honor. In what way was the fight between the boys "an honorable thing" for both Marv and Benjie?

Marv had been dishonored by Benjie's taunt, and the fight gave him a chance to regain self-respect. Benjie, so small and weak that everyone called him Mouse, was able to gain stature and respect in spite of losing the fight, because he courageously confronted his problem. The proof of this new respect is that Ezzie, at the end of the book, looks at Mouse and wonders if he had actually gotten taller and calls him "Benjie," not Mouse.

The 18th Emergency

by Betsy Byars

CHOOSE ONE WRITING ACTIVITY THAT INTERESTS YOU.

A. Everybody needs to feel respected. When a person's dignity is damaged, that person must regain it or lose a sense of honor. This is what happened in the conflict between Benjie and Marv. Create a story in which a young person challenges an adult in such a way that the adult feels dishonored. You must figure out a way to resolve this conflict. The adult and the young person must both have a sense of self-worth at the end of your story.

B. Fear of the unknown creates suspense. Develop a story in which you have a character exploring an unknown place or confronting an unknown situation. Stretch it out so that the reader feels anxious right along with your character. Devices Byars used that you might want to consider are

1. keeping information from the reader until the end,

2. having a series of near misses, and

3. making the reader aware of time ticking away, especially in a situation where time is limited.

Writer's Triangle © 1989

The Great Gilly Hopkins

by Katherine Paterson
(Crowell, 1978,
ISBN 0-290-03837-2;
in paperback,
Avon/Camelot, 1979,
ISBN 0-380-45963-9).
Realistic Fiction.

Filmstrip set
(Cat. #394-65973-2)
31-1/2 min. VHS
(Cat. #676-27835-3),
and listening cassette
are available from Random
House Media, Dept. 437,
400 Hahn Road,
Westminster, MD
21157-9939.

Summary: Gilly is a foster child who has been bouncing from family to family. She is highly intelligent, enormously angry, and determined to contact her real mother, whom she fantasizes will make her whole life fine. As the book opens, she is being taken to her new placement with an uneducated, fat, kind woman—Maime Trotter—who also cares for William Ernest, a slow, timid child, and for Mr. Randolph, a blind, black neighbor. Trotter's kindness and directness win Gilly over, and the love she finds in this household helps her when she must accept that her mother doesn't want her and she will have to leave Trotter to live with her grandmother.

Comments: *Gilly* is a lively book, written with humor and great insight. It includes some mild "language" as well as difficult issues such as parental neglect and racial prejudice. It is all done delicately and with good taste, however, never straying far from the theme that love is the most powerful force.

Name _____ Room _____

The Great Gilly Hopkins

by Katherine Paterson

**Meet with your discussion group before you begin
reading and talk about how you would behave if you
were a foster child and it seemed that no one cared
about you.**

As you read, think about

- how Gilly's rebellious behavior affects her and the
  people around her
- what the basic problem or conflict is
- how Katherine Paterson uses unusual characters and
  language to make the book exciting

Schedule

Fact Check Test _____

Discussion _____

First Draft Due _____

Final Draft Due _____

Notes

_____

_____

_____

_____

_____

Writer's Triangle © 1989

Fact Check Test

The Great Gilly Hopkins
by Katherine Paterson

1. What did Gilly put under the door handle of the car?

   _____

2. What did Gilly and the boys fight over her first day at school?

   _____

3. What handicap did Mr. Randolph have?

   _____

4. What did Gilly make that made Miss Harris angry?

   _____

5. Where did Gilly find the money in Mr. Randolph's house?

   _____

6. How did Gilly contact her mother?

   _____

7. Why did Trotter make Gilly work in the house and help William Ernest with schoolwork?

   _____

8. What did Gilly teach William Ernest in addition to school subjects?

   _____

9. Why did Gilly have to cook the Thanksgiving turkey?

   _____

10. With whom did Gilly live at the end of the book?

    _____

The Great Gilly Hopkins
by Katherine Paterson

1. What did Gilly put under the door handle of the car?

    bubble gum or gum

2. What did Gilly and the boys fight over her first day at school?

    basketball or ball

3. What handicap did Mr. Randolph have?

    He was blind.

4. What did Gilly make that made Miss Harris angry?

    a card that made fun of blacks

5. Where did Gilly find the money in Mr. Randolph's house?

    in the bookcase

6. How did Gilly contact her mother?

    sent her a letter

7. Why did Trotter make Gilly work in the house and help William Ernest with schoolwork?

    repay stolen money

8. What did Gilly teach William Ernest in addition to school subjects?

    how to stick up for himself; how to make airplanes

9. Why did Gilly have to cook the Thanksgiving turkey?

    everyone else was sick, or Trotter was sick

10. With whom did Gilly live at the end of the book?

    her grandmother

The Great Gilly Hopkins

by Katherine Paterson

Note: Page numbers here are for the Avon/Camelot paperback edition.

SETTING

The setting of *The Great Gilly Hopkins* keeps us focused on important elements in the story.

1. How does Paterson use the setting, Trotter's house, to contribute to the conflict Gilly has with her situation?

Gilly is used to orderly houses, probably richer environments, and bigger rooms. This house makes her feel more resentful.

2. How does the author use Trotter's house to show us Trotter's personality?

The house is sloppy, dusty, and uncared for, but it is comfortable and can accommodate anyone who comes to it.

CHARACTER

1. Gilly is furious that she has to go to Trotter's foster home. What techniques does Paterson use in Chapter 1 to show us that Gilly is angry?

▮ Gilly's behavior: blowing bubbles and ignoring Miss Ellis, putting gum under the door handle, giving a "barracuda smile," scaring William Ernest.

▮ Gilly's thoughts: "Nobody wants to tangle with the great Galadriel Hopkins. I am too clever and too hard to manage. Gruesome Gilly, they call me."

▮ Gilly's mental images: "With her uplifted left foot, she was shoving the next foster mother square in the mouth."

▮ Miss Ellis's comments: "Please try to behave" and "For Pete's sake."

2. **Authors use minor characters to show major characters' development. Paterson made Trotter fat, William Ernest slow, and Miss Harris and Mr. Randolph black and handicapped. How did Gilly's reaction to these characters change and what did the change tell us about Gilly?**

Each represents a prejudice of Gilly's that she overcomes by learning to care for the people who possess the trait. Gilly's prejudices are one of her defenses against her own feelings of inferiority and insecurity.

3. **Paterson makes Gilly's rebelliousness a central feature of the book. In the early part of the book, Gilly rebels to protect herself from more rejection at home and at school. Tell some examples of this.**

Fear of rejection by yet another foster home makes her hostile to Trotter; fear of rejection in her new school makes her try to control school so that they can't push her around. (See pp. 19, 21-23, 44-45, 53-55.) Feeling like a number, not important to anyone, she distinguishes herself, although negatively. (See p. 55.)

4. **What does Paterson tell us about Gilly's feelings about herself when she stops being rebellious at the end of the book?**

She feels loved and secure; she doesn't need to protect herself anymore.

PLOT

1. **Every story has a major conflict. What is the conflict in this book?**

Gilly wants what she can't have: her mother.

2. **How does Paterson develop sympathy for Gilly even when she's being bad?**

We learn about how she's been bounced around, especially by the family that seemed to really love her and then moved to Florida and left her. She's got a lot going for her—she's smart, perceptive, and proud—and most touching to the reader, she's vulnerable.

3. **How does the author make Gilly realize she is worthwhile?**

People forgive her: Trotter keeps her after she steals, William Ernest seems to really want her to stay, Mr. Randolph doesn't deliver a sermon when she returns the money, and Miss Harris forgives her racial slur. People need her: she teaches William Ernest self-confidence and helps him read, she reads to Mr. Randolph and guides him to the house, and she helps when everyone is sick, even cooking Thanksgiving dinner. She also feels needed by her grandma, who is all alone.

Writer's Triangle © 1989

4. **Gilly's letter to her mother sets a chain of events in motion that ultimately makes things happen in a way Gilly doesn't like. Why do you think Paterson chose to set this chain of events in motion and not to have a completely happy ending (such as the perfect mother comes and loves her and takes her home)?**

This ending enables Paterson to show Gilly's development into a more responsible, realistic person who begins to understand other peoples' needs and points of view. She now faces the reality of her situation and gives up daydreaming about Courtney. She is also concerned about her grandmother and recognizes that her grandmother needs her. Perhaps Paterson also wants us to consider whether Gilly might eventually be happier with her real family.

LITERARY TECHNIQUE

1. **One way an author makes a plot interesting is by using a technique called *foreshadowing*. Clues are given to the reader about something that is going to happen later.**

   A. What clues do we get that Courtney doesn't want Gilly?

   ▌ Miss Ellis's eyebrows twitch when Gilly asks questions about Courtney (p. 15)

   ▌ Shortness of Courtney's post card, which is her first communication in ages (p. 28)

   ▌ Gilly hasn't seen Courtney since she was three (p. 29)

   ▌ Courtney never answered when Miss Ellis wrote about Gilly's move from the Nevinses. For eight years she had never come to see her (pp. 95-96)

   B. Why doesn't Paterson have Gilly understand that Courtney doesn't want her?

   It builds tension: we see the trouble coming for Gilly, although Gilly doesn't.

2. **Another way an author makes a book interesting is by using vivid language. For example, when Gilly feels emotional, she says, "This was not the time to start dissolving like hot Jello," and when William Ernest begs Gilly to come home, Paterson writes, "The ice on her frozen brain rumbled and cracked."**

   On the Vivid Images Worksheet are several more samples of Paterson's use of language.

Vivid Images Worksheet

The Great Gilly Hopkins
by Katherine Paterson

Read the examples of Paterson's vivid language below. Following her patterns, see if you can create vivid images of your own by replacing the underlined phrases.

1. "Mr. Randolph, you could flatter the_ stripe off a polecat."

   _____

2. The woman lay there, <u>flapping on her back like a giant overturned tortoise.</u>

   _____

3. Listening to that woman was like <u>licking melted ice cream off the carton.</u>

   _____

4. . . . but she felt heavier with each step—like <u>a condemned prisoner walking an endless last mile.</u>

   _____

5. He straightened his thin shoulders and marched up the stairs as though he were <u>President of the United States.</u>

   _____

6. Her voice was Southern but smooth, like <u>silk to Trotter's burlap.</u>

   _____

7. . . . her mouth going dry <u>as a stale soda cracker</u> . . .

   _____

8. . . . her heart carried on like <u>the entire percussion section of a marching band doing "The Stars and Stripes Forever."</u>

   _____

The Great Gilly Hopkins

by Katherine Paterson

CHOOSE ONE WRITING ACTIVITY THAT INTERESTS YOU.

As you learned from your reading and from the Vivid Images Worksheet, a good author makes language interesting by making clever comparisons. In either of the following writing activities, you will need to include comparisons of your own. It is important to try to compare people or things in unusual but appropriate ways as Paterson does. Be sure your comparison makes sense and helps the reader understand your idea. When making comparisons, it is helpful to think about what things act like, look like, smell like, feel like, and perhaps even taste like.

A. Write a scene in which you have a character (or yourself) go to one of the following: a hospital, a carnival, or a summer camp. Help your readers visualize the scene by including at least three interesting comparisons.

B. Create a scene in which two very different characters are trying to capture the attention of the most popular boy or girl in the school. As you describe each of the three characters, make your description vivid for your readers by using clever comparisons.

Hazel Rye

by Vera and Bill Cleaver
(Harper & Row/
Lippincott Jr., 1983,
ISBN 0-397-31951-7;
in paperback,
Harper/Trophy, 1985,
ISBN 0-06-440156-1).
Realistic Fiction.

Summary: Hazel Rye can barely read or write and has failed sixth grade. This doesn't bother her father, however. His education is no better than hers, and he has plenty of money to take her out to dinner all the time and to buy a big Cadillac to drive her around. She daydreams about quitting school so that she can drive a taxi and make $300 a week. She'd also like to fix up her run-down orange grove and then sell it for lots of money. When Felder Poole and his family arrive in town, it looks as if her dream may come true. Instead, her dream changes. His knowledge, diligence, and love of growing things teaches Hazel that there are more important things in the world than money. Hazel's new attitude and new goals cause a strain between herself and her father. Uneducated himself, he tries to keep her at his level and jealously guards her relationships with other people. Hazel's triumph is that she is able to grow within the parameters her father sets for her.

Comments: The Cleavers have created several memorable characters, an interesting and informative setting, and a good story. The characters speak with distinct voices. The story lends itself to discussion about conflicts, goals, and turning points.

Prereading Focus

Hazel Rye

by Vera and Bill Cleaver

Meet with your discussion group before you begin reading and talk about what you think your life would be like if you didn't know how to read.

As you read, think about

- ▐ what kind of influence Hazel's father is on her life
- ▐ what influence the Pooles have on Hazel
- ▐ how the Cleavers show differences in characters by giving them distinctive speech patterns (for example, notice how Hazel's speech is different from her father's)

Schedule

Fact Check Test _____

Discussion _____

First Draft Due _____

Final Draft Due _____

Notes

_____

_____

_____

_____

_____

Writer's Triangle © 1989

Name _____   Room _____

Hazel Rye
by Vera and Bill Cleaver

1. Who reminded Hazel of a pioneer lady who might get out and help the mules pull the wagon?

   _____

2. Why did the Pooles clean the Ryes' kitchen?

   _____

3. What did Hazel do to Felder's puffball?

   _____

4. What did Felder first ask Hazel to do in the grove?

   _____

5. What did Jewel Poole love to do that Hazel couldn't do?

   _____

6. Hazel's father said she could not help Felder in the grove. How did she trick him into changing his mind?

   _____

7. Why couldn't Hazel and her father build the model boat?

   _____

8. What did the children get from Mr. Bartlett to sell in the park?

   _____

9. Who told the policeman that the young man had robbed the children?

   _____

10. What did Felder leave Hazel when he moved away?

   _____

Hazel Rye

by Vera and Bill Cleaver

1. Who reminded Hazel of a pioneer lady who might get out and help the mules pull the wagon?

   Mrs. Poole

2. Why did the Pooles clean the Ryes' kitchen?

   in exchange for food and money

3. What did Hazel do to Felder's puffball?

   cut into it

4. What did Felder first ask Hazel to do in the grove?

   hoe, or dig, around trees

5. What did Jewel Poole love to do that Hazel couldn't do?

   read

6. Hazel's father said she could not help Felder in the grove. How did she trick him into changing his mind?

   She said she watched TV all day and saw a movie about a little girl who set houses on fire and another one with a lot of kissing.

7. Why couldn't Hazel and her father build the model boat?

   They couldn't read the directions.

8. What did the children get from Mr. Bartlett to sell in the park?

   plants, or flowers

9. Who told the policeman that the young man had robbed the children?

   the mayor

10. What did Felder leave Hazel when he moved away?

    a jar of seeds

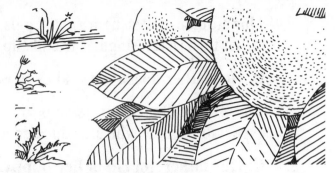

Hazel Rye

by Vera and Bill Cleaver

Note: Page numbers here are for the Harper/Trophy paperback edition.

PLOT AND CONFLICT

1. In this book the Cleavers present a struggle between two main characters. Which characters are in the most conflict throughout the book?

Hazel and her father

2. What are some of the things Hazel wants to do that her father won't allow?

Hazel wants to get her ears pierced, rent the house, and sell flowers.

3. Ultimately, Mr. Rye lets her get her ears pierced, lets her rent the house, and lets her develop her grove, which shows us that he doesn't care a lot about these issues. What is the real issue that the Cleavers want us to see motivating Mr. Rye?

Mr. Rye wants to keep Hazel's affection and loyalty for himself.

4. The Cleavers never have Mr. Rye say that he wants Hazel's attention for himself, although they show it in several scenes. How do the following scenes illustrate Mr Rye's determination to keep Hazel's attention and affection for himself?

A. Hazel's mother leaves for an extended trip and they don't stop her.

Mr. Rye doesn't seem to mind. As long as he has Hazel's company, he doesn't miss other people.

B. Her father encourages her poor schoolwork.

He wants to keep her uneducated, so she won't become "better" than he is and want to leave him.

C. Her father allows slovenly house management.

This attitude makes them a team, pals. He takes her out to eat all the time rather then risk losing her friendship by making her work.

D. Her father doesn't want her to work with Felder or Mr. Bartlett.

This shows that he is jealous of her contact with other people—especially people who are educated and might pull her away from him.

E. Her father got rid of her puppy.

Again, he was jealous. She really loved the puppy, and her father didn't like losing her attention.

INTERACTION OF PLOT AND CHARACTER

1. What are the Cleavers trying to tell us about Mr. Rye when they show him trying to keep Hazel from going out into the world?

He's insecure and lonely. He is uneducated and doesn't seem to be close to his wife or to other people.

2. Why do the Cleavers put Felder in the story? How do his personality and interests affect other characters?

He is a catalyst who brings about the changes in Hazel. In the beginning she is lazy, uninterested in school or learning, and without friends. Felder's enthusiasm for growing things, his intelligence and curiosity, and his diligence and dependability show her another way. At the end of the book, she displays many of his qualities and is determined to improve herself by doing housework, farming, and learning to read.

CHARACTER

1. How do the Cleavers let us know that Hazel and her father are uneducated?

Their lack of education is apparent in their language and in Mr. Rye's reading comics instead of other parts of the paper. In the scene where they try to read the model directions, we see how poor reading skills affect them both.

2. Why do the Cleavers make the Pooles so different from the Ryes?

▋ Making the Pooles educated, lively, and hardworking provides a vivid contrast to the Ryes, who are uneducated, apathetic, and slothful.

▋ The difference enables Felder to act as a catalyst for Hazel's character development.

3. You'd expect to dislike a person who tries to hold another back, keep her from having friends, and control her for his own needs. But we don't hate Mr. Rye. How do the Cleavers make us like him in spite of his selfish behavior?

■ He obviously loves Hazel. He brings her things, likes to talk with her, and goes out to the movies with her.

■ He wants Hazel to be happy. When she sulks, he tries to make up with her. He doesn't want her to do just anything he says.

■ He's a kind man and a good, hardworking citizen. "Millard Rye was a good husband and provider, didn't cuss or drink or smoke, ate what was placed in front of him with little or no complaint, and didn't snore or grind his teeth in his sleep. He was a carpenter of good reputation who usually employed one or two helpers and every morning rose and cooked his own breakfast and Hazel's. All of his days except Sundays were spent at heavy labor" (p. 7).

SETTING

1. How do the Cleavers use the main setting, a citrus grove in Florida, to make the book more interesting?

■ We learn a lot about growing things.

■ We learn about the struggle people have with this occupation.

2. How do the Cleavers use one of the settings, Vannie Lee's house, to show us a change in Hazel?

Hazel's new involvement with her grove makes her contemptuous of all the material things that Vannie has collected. Note especially the silk flowers that Vannie brags about; Hazel and Felder are more interested in growing real ones.

LANGUAGE

The Cleavers use colorful, picturesque language to make their writing vivid.

1. Can you identify the person or thing each of the following sentences describes?

A. I had me a teacher who always made me feel as guilty as a dog at a icebox when I didn't know the answer. (p.4)

Mr. Rye

B. . . . as homely as a cucumber and possessed of a nervous, slipshod nature. (p. 8)

Mrs. Rye

C. . . . most of all as useless as a raincoat to a whale. (p. 21)

the small amount of rain and food that the grove gets

D. That suit she's got on today fits her like a drink of water. (p. 47)

Vannie Lee

E. . . . dottings of freakish growths, some with dagger spikes and others with octopus arms. (p. 75)

Mr. Bartlett's plants

2. How does this kind of language extend our understanding?

Simile and metaphor comparisons let us see interesting characteristics of something or someone. The author makes a connection we probably wouldn't make ourselves.

ENDING

1. Do you like the way the book ended?

Answers will vary.

2. Why do you think the Cleavers did not have the Pooles remain in the house and Felder continue to help Hazel?

They want to show that the change in Hazel isn't just Felder's actions; she'll stand taller and stronger even without him.

Hazel Rye

by Vera and Bill Cleaver

CHOOSE ONE WRITING ACTIVITY THAT INTERESTS YOU.

A. One of the tasks of writers is to give readers information about past events in a natural and interesting way. Dialogue between characters who really need to know about each other is one way to accomplish this. Write a scene that takes place ten years after the end of the book. Have Hazel meet Felder Poole in your scene. You can decide where and how this meeting will take place. It could be on a college campus, at an auction where an orange grove is being sold, or at a sports event. In their conversation reveal what has happened to each of them since they last saw each other. Think about their schooling, occupations, and other family members.

B. Conflict between parents and children is not uncommon. Develop a scene in which a child wants to go to summer camp, play a sport that's dangerous, or have an unsuitable friend, but the parent says "no." Think about what the problem is and what steps you might take to solve it if it were your problem. Write from the point of view of the child so you can include your feelings as well as the dialogue that takes place between you and your parents.

Ida Early Comes Over the Mountain

by Robert Burch
(Viking, 1980,
ISBN 0-670-39169-7;
in paperback,
Avon/Camelot, 1982,
ISBN 0-380-57091-2).
Realistic Fiction/Humor.

Summary: The Sutton children have lost their mother and are being cared for by bossy, overbearing Aunt Earnestine when Ida Early arrives on their doorstep looking for work. Tall and homely, with a warm, generous spirit and a quick laugh, she brings joy back into the house with her tall stories and delight in games. The crisis of the book comes when children in the schoolyard mock her and neither Randall nor Ellen come to her defense. Profoundly hurt, she turns serious and tries to become less funny-looking. She also sends signals that she will be leaving. The children write her a letter of apology, which they tuck into her knapsack for her to find after she leaves, and Randall invites her to perform rope tricks with him in the school show. Both measures are successful, and the book ends on a cheerful note, with Ida Early back to her old self and returned to the Sutton household.

Comments: Many funny and warm scenes and a memorable character in Ida Early make this an easy read. The underlying, serious dilemma of choosing worthwhile values, such as loyalty, over surface values, such as appearance, gives it a deeper dimension as well.

Prereading Focus

Ida Early Comes Over the Mountain
by Robert Burch

   Meet with your discussion group before you begin reading and talk about what you would do if the kids you wanted to get along with at school made fun of someone you cared about.

As you read, think about

▌ how Ida Early's sense of humor makes life better
▌ how Ida Early's physical appearance affects the story

Schedule

Fact Check Test _____

Discussion _____

First Draft Due _____

Final Draft Due _____

Notes

_____

_____

_____

_____

_____

Name _____ Room _____

Fact Check Test

Ida Early Comes Over the Mountain
by Robert Burch

1. What did Randall decide Ida Early reminded him of when he first saw her?

   _____

2. Ida Early's first job at the Suttons was to cook the stew. Who actually cooked it?

   _____

3. What game could the young twins play better than Ida Early and Ellen and Randall?

   _____

4. Listening to Ida Early's stories, Randall felt they tended to be _____ .

5. Ida Early bragged about being a lion tamer. What farm animal did she tame?

   _____

6. Where did Noon say Ida Early belonged after she beat him knocking over the dolls at the carnival?

   _____

7. When Kathy Alice joined the Country Club, her password was "bucket of _____ ."

8. Why did Ida Early go to school the first time?

   _____

9. What game did Randall and Ellen buy Ida Early to make her feel that they liked her?

   _____

10. Ida Early saved Daisy's life at the Wild West show because she lassoed the _____ .

Ida Early Comes Over the Mountain

by Robert Burch

1. What did Randall decide Ida Early reminded him of when he first saw her?

scarecrow

2. Ida Early's first job at the Suttons was to cook the stew. Who actually cooked it?

the children

3. What game could the young twins play better than Ida Early and Ellen and Randall?

tiddlywinks

4. Listening to Ida Early's stories, Randall felt they tended to be _____.

lies or exaggerations

5. Ida Early bragged about being a lion tamer. What farm animal did she tame?

pig

6. Where did Noon say Ida Early belonged after she beat him knocking over dolls at the carnival?

freak show

7. When Kathy Alice joined the Country Club, her password was "bucket of _____."

mud

8. Why did Ida Early go to school the first time?

the twins wouldn't go without her

9. What game did Randall and Ellen buy Ida Early to make her feel that they liked her?

checkers

10. Ida Early saved Daisy's life at the Wild West show because she lassoed the _____.

bear

Ida Early Comes Over the Mountain

by Robert Burch

Note: Page numbers here are for the Avon/Camelot paperback edition.

CHARACTER

1. One of the skills in writing well is being able to create distinctive, interesting characters. How does Robert Burch make Ida Early distinctive? In what ways is she different from other people?

▮ Her appearance is odd. She is tall, like a scarecrow, wears odd clothes, and is very plain.

▮ She tells big lies about herself to entertain the children, and truth and fantasy in her life begin to blur.

▮ She has unexpected and delightful skills, such as roping or being able to throw her sweater from anywhere in the room and have it land on the hatrack.

▮ She's clever about getting the kids to pitch in and help with her chores, as when she gets them to cook stew while she plays tiddlywinks, but she is also good-natured about helping others, as when she does Randall's milking for him.

▮ She is not in awe of Aunt Earnestine and is able to defy her without appearing to do so.

2. In a good book, the characters change; they grow, mature, learn something. What important lessons do Ellen and Randall learn in the course of the book?

▮ It is important to be loyal, even if it means exposing yourself to some embarrassment.

▮ Personality and good character are more important than physical appearance.

3. Aunt Earnestine and Aunt Myrtle are comic characters. They don't mean to be funny; in fact, they take themselves very seriously. However, their behavior and the reactions of other characters

make us laugh. What are they like and what things does Robert Burch have them do or say that help create funny scenes?

Aunt Earnestine is likened to a battleship (p. 7). She is straight-laced and stuffy and therefore horrified by Ida Early's antics. Since the whole family, including Mr. Sutton, conspires to protect Ida Early, Aunt Earnestine gets to look ridiculous. When she tells Ida that "the comic strips will wait; the dishes won't" (p. 26), Ida turns it into a big joke, saying comics get thrown out but dirty dishes never go away. When Earnestine suggests that Aunt Myrtle could come with Kathy Alice, Mr. Sutton says, "Deliver me!" When they do come for a Sunday visit, Kathy Alice is such a spoiled brat and Aunt Myrtle so critical that we are delighted when the game of Country Club is turned on Kathy Alice. We know the children will not get in trouble because Aunt Myrtle is so firm in being bossy—without knowing what she is talking about—that when she insists that the older children should not interfere, even Mr. Sutton decides to let Kathy Alice get her bucket of mud.

4. How does Burch show us that Ida is profoundly hurt after the schoolyard incident?

She goes off for a day and when she comes back, she speaks in a flat voice, says hello instead of howdy; her eyes lack their usual spark and she has a downcast expression. Although she tries to fix herself up by buying a dress and women's shoes and curling her hair, there is no joy in her and she doesn't laugh or joke with the family.

5. How does Burch show us that Ida is back to her old self at the end of the book?

Ida vrooms in on a motorcycle, has a big grin, throws her jacket across the room, lands it on the hatrack, and says she misses her true *friends*. Then she tells a big lie about walking on the wings of airplanes and lights a match on the seat of her pants as she did when she first came.

PLOT

1. What is the Sutton family's problem?

Mrs. Sutton died, leaving them without a wife and mother.

2. Authors sometimes put their characters in a threatening situation. This is a device that helps hold the reader's interest. Most of the time this is serious and we are worried for the characters. In *Ida Early*,

however, the story is humorous, so the threat can't be very danger-ous. What is the comic threat that hangs over the children, relieved only when Ida Early comes to stay?

That one of their well-meaning but bossy and unpleasant aunts will move in.

3. **Because their "problem" is solved in the opening pages of the book, Burch has to create a crisis that will reactivate their problem or create a new one. How does he do this?**

He sets up a situation in which Ida Early is so upset that she will leave. (This is the schoolyard incident in which the children mock her and neither Randall nor Ellen defend her.) When she does leave, we are unsure whether she will return.

4. **Foreshadowing is a technique writers use to give the reader a hint of what is coming. How did the scene at the carnival, in which Noon says, "I think you belong in a freak show," foreshadow the encoun-ter Ida has with the children in the schooyard?**

When Noon says something cruel and laughs at her, we get a sense of how ignorant people in the outside world might react to her. This prepares us for Dan, Daisy, and Fay calling cruel things to her and laughing.

5. **In what way did the two incidents differ? Why was Ida Early so much more upset after the schoolyard incident than she was after the carnival incident?**

After Noon attacked her, Clay told Ida Early that he didn't think she was funny-looking; in fact, he said she was prettier than anybody in the world. But in the schoolyard, Randall and Ellen were embarrassed and let the children taunt her. By the time Randall made Dan drop the stone he was going to throw, it was too late for Ida to know.

6. **What purpose does the "Rope Tricks" chapter serve in the plot? Why is this chapter so important and satisfying?**

It is the point at which Ida Early proves herself worthy in front of all the children who mocked her.

SETTING

Ida Early Comes Over the Mountain is set in rural Georgia during the Depression. How does Robert Burch use this setting to enhance his plot? What things happen in the story that are directly related both to the time and the place?

◼ The story's being set in the Depression makes it believable that Ida Early would be walking around the mountains looking for work. It also makes her clothes believable.

◼ The rural setting isolates the family, so that the Sutton children don't have to face outsiders' ridicule of Ida until Burch is ready to create the crisis in the schoolyard.

◼ Certain incidents are directly related to farm life. For example, Archie puts himself in danger by grabbing one of Mayflower's piglets. The game of Country Club is played in the barn and uses farming props, such as hay and burlap bags.

◼ Because the story takes place in the mountains, it is believable that someone would have a bear to bring to the Wild West show.

Ida Early Comes Over the Mountain

by Robert Burch

CHOOSE ONE WRITING ACTIVITY THAT INTERESTS YOU.

A. Before Robert Burch could write I*da Early Comes Over the Mountain,* he had to have a clear picture in his mind of what Ida Early looked like and how she would behave. Invent an interesting-looking character. Draw a picture of your character, including as many details as you can. Then write a description of how your character looks as well as some things about his or her personality.

B. Think about the ways Burch makes the aunts in this story comic. The contrast between the way they take themselves seriously and the way other people see them as rude and bossy is funny. Create a humorous scene in which you have a character unaware of the effect he or she has on the other characters. The character can be someone who thinks he or she is impressing people who in fact aren't impressed, or someone who is telling a lie, thinking he or she is getting away with it, when in fact the other characters see that it is a lie. You may use your own idea instead, if you have a different comic character situation in mind.

One-eyed Cat

by Paula Fox
(Bradbury Press, 1984,
ISBN 0-02-735540-3;
in paperback,
Dell/Yearling, 1986,
ISBN 0-440-46641-5).
Realistic Fiction.

Filmstrip set
(Cat. #676-31276-4) and
listening cassette
(Cat. #676-31284-5) are
available from Random
House Media, Dept. 437,
400 Hahn Road,
Westminster, MD
21157-9939.

Summary: Ned Wallis, son of a minister and an invalid mother, receives a gun from his Uncle Hilary for his eleventh birthday. His parents direct him not to use it, and it is hidden in the attic. Ned sneaks it out one night and shoots at a moving shadow. When he later sees a one-eyed cat in the neighborhood, he is sure he is responsible. Ned's elderly friend, with whom he cared for the cat, helps with a forgiving hand squeeze shortly before he dies, and Ned is finally able to confess to his mother and find some peace about it. In addition to working through his guilt and fear about the cat, Ned must cope with his housekeeper, the marvelously awful Mrs. Scallop, a character worthy of Charles Dickens.

Comments: This is an intense and riveting story despite the measured pace and quiet setting. Characterization is outstanding.

Prereading Focus

One-eyed Cat
by Paula Fox

Meet with your discussion group before you begin reading and talk about what you would do to try to put things right if your carelessness made you injure an animal.

As you read, think about

▮ how keeping a secret from his parents affects Ned's feelings about himself and his relationships with other people

▮ which characters in the book are concerned about being good and how it affects them and their relationships with each other

Schedule

Fact Check Test _____

Discussion _____

First Draft Due _____

Final Draft Due _____

Notes

_____

_____

_____

_____

_____

Writer's Triangle © 1989

| Fact Check Test | |

One-eyed Cat
by Paula Fox

1. What kind of food did the ladies of the church usually send the Wallis family?

_____

2. Why didn't Ned's family live in the parsonage?

_____

3. What chores did Ned do for Mr. Scully?

_____

4. What did Uncle Hilary give Ned for his birthday?

_____

5. What animal did Billy Gaskell threaten to harm?

_____

6. What did Uncle Hilary's friend cook for him the day he got out of the hospital?

_____

7. What happened to Mr. Scully?

_____

8. What important thing was Ned unable to do when he got sick at Christmas?

_____

9. What did Mr. Scully do to show Ned that he understood about the cat and did not think
   he was a "bad" person?

_____

10. Where did Mrs. Scallop end up working?

_____

11. What good thing happened to Ned's mother at the end of the book?

_____

One-eyed Cat

by Paula Fox

1. What kind of food did the ladies of the church usually send to the Wallis family?

   desserts

2. Why didn't Ned's family live in the parsonage?

   They really loved the family home, where his father grew up and where his mother had a good view of the Hudson River.

3. What chores did Ned do for Mr. Scully?

   bringing the mail, washing his dishes, sweeping out the kitchen, bringing in some wood, helping him go through boxes

4. What did Uncle Hilary give Ned for his birthday?

   a gun

5. What animal did Billy Gaskell threaten to harm?

   a snake

6. What did Uncle Hilary's friend cook for him the day he got out of the hospital?

   two boiled potatoes

7. What happened to Mr. Scully?

   He had a stroke, went to the hospital, then to the nursing home, and finally he died.

8. What important thing was Ned unable to do when he got sick at Christmas?

   feed the cat

9. What did Mr. Scully do to show Ned that he understood about the cat and did not think he was a "bad" person?

   He pressed Ned's hand.

10. Where did Mrs. Scallop end up working?

    the Waterville Nursing Home

11. What good thing happened to Ned's mother at the end of the book?

    A new treatment—gold salts— was helping her, and she was able to walk again.

Writer's Triangle © 1989

Discussion Guide

One-eyed Cat

by Paula Fox

Note: Page numbers here are for the Dell/Yearling paperback edition.

SETTING

Why did Paula Fox set this story in a rural area during the Great Depression?

A rural setting is the most reasonable one in which Ned could shoot a wild cat and care for it during the winter. The rural setting enables him to become friendly with an elderly neighbor and share the care of the cat with him and not have his parents aware of any of it. It also physically isolates the family more than a city or suburban setting would have. This, as well as the mother's sickness, brings the family members closer and intensifies their relationships.

Since the story takes place during the Depression, there is not a lot of money, so the cat could not be healed with an expensive trip to the vet.

Another way the time is important is that the story takes place at the time a treatment for rheumatoid arthritis was discovered.

PLOT

1. Paula Fox does not tell us why Ned gets the gun out of the attic and sneaks it into the woods to shoot it. She tells us enough about Ned and his situation, however, so that we can guess. Why do you think he takes the gun and shoots it?

Uncle Hilary's giving him the gun makes him feel like an adult. The gun seems to give him a sense of power, which he likes but is not ready to control. His father understands this, which is why he wants Ned to wait until he is older. Unfortunately, treating him as "not ready" makes Ned feel humiliated. The humiliation and disappointment with his father's decision probably makes him angry, and he acts impulsively.

2. The plot that Paula Fox has created does not have a lot of conflict between characters, although there is some. The main conflict is

within Ned, caused by his decision not to tell his family about the cat. Why does he lie to them? Why does the lie cause such pain?

At first, he is afraid. He has disobeyed them and done something wrong. Then when he realizes that he may have injured the cat, he is ashamed. He doesn't want to lose their love, and he is afraid that is what might happen if he confessed. On the other hand, his family is honest, and he has obviously been open with them. Having a guilty secret to carry puts a big barrier between them. They sense it and he certainly does too. As time goes on, he tells more and more lies to cover up, and this digs him in deeper. It becomes harder to tell the truth.

CHARACTER

1. **Although they are generally gracious to each other, we can see that Paula has created some tension between Uncle Hilary and Ned's father. What do you think is the cause of this tension, and why do you think Fox included it?**

Uncle Hilary and Reverend Wallis are very different. Uncle Hilary seems carefree. He has no responsibilities—perhaps we could even say he lives a self-centered existence. He travels all over the globe, seems to be a lot of fun, and brings joy to the household whenever he visits. This sets up a clear contrast to the somber, devoted highly responsible reverend, who is so selfless and good that both his wife and son are somewhat intimidated by him.

2. **Why does Ned's father's goodness keep Ned from sharing his problem with him?**

Ned is afraid he'll disappoint his father. He wants his father to think well of him.

3. **Why does Fox have Ned's mother share the story of how she ran away from home when he was a young child?**

She wants Mrs. Wallis to show Ned that she understands and forgives his imperfections because she is imperfect herself. By telling him that she was afraid of his father's goodness, she tells him that she understands how he is intimidated by it; sharing her mistakes tells him that it is all right to make mistakes.

His father being there to greet them at the door when they return from this revealing talk and saying, "I'm so glad you've come home," shows them as well as the reader that he loves them and needs them both and perhaps understands that they've "been away" emotionally, as well as on a walk.

Writer's Triangle © 1989

4. Why did Paula Fox make Ned's mother an invalid?

She sets up a contrast between her physical helplessness and her spiritual strength. It is her sense of humor, her insight, and her directness that help Ned through his troubles. It also makes him protective of her, so it is more believable that he not tell her about the cat until she is well.

5. After Mrs. Scallop has upset Ned by telling him that Mr. Scully would have to go to an old folks home, Ned's mother says of Mrs. Scallop ". . . you must beware of people who wear their hearts on their sleeves; it's not the natural place to keep your heart—it turns rusty and thin, and it leaves you hollow inside" (p. 72). What does Mrs. Wallis mean? Do you think her description fits Mrs. Scallop well?

She means that Mrs. Scallop is not bighearted, that she is not generous or warm. Because of this, she is hollow (unhappy) inside. This description does seem to fit Mrs. Scallop, who is a bully and cruel and mean-spirited. She brags about herself because she is hungry for compliments she never gets, and she gets even by being hostile.

SYMBOLS

Authors sometimes create people, objects, or incidents that have more than one role in the story. They have a literal meaning; that is, they are what they seem to be, but they also mean something more, either to a character in the story or to the reader. When this happens, they become symbols.

1. What does the cat symbolize to Ned?

It symbolizes his "badness" (his irresponsibility and the lying he does to cover it) for which he must atone by caring for the cat. At the end, when he sees the cat playing and when he confesses to his mother and she shows that she forgives him, he can finally put it behind him.

2. What does the cat represent to Mr. Scully?

It seems to represent life. He says (p. 142), "When you get to be my age, the strength of life in a living creature can't help but gladden your heart." When he sees the cat survive against the odds, he is encouraged for himself in the face of his own diminished strength.

3. What does Billy's attack on the snake mean to Ned?

It is a replay of the incident with the cat. Here it is Billy who is thoughtlessly cruel, the way Ned had been to the cat.

One-eyed Cat
by Paula Fox

CHOOSE ONE WRITING ACTIVITY THAT INTERESTS YOU.

A. *One-eyed Cat* is the story of a boy's feelings of guilt over something he has done. Think about something you have done that made you feel guilty, or if you wish, imagine something you could have done. Tell about what you did (or could have done), how it made you feel, what problems it caused you, and how you resolved your problems.

B. Paula Fox has created a supremely unpleasant character in Mrs. Scallop. She wants us to experience just how mean, dominating, and oppressive Mrs. Scallop is. To do this, Fox doesn't tell us what Mrs. Scallop is like; she shows us. She has created incidents in which Mrs. Scallop makes life unpleasant for the people around her, so we can feel her personality just the way the characters in the book feel it. Write a story in which your main character has to deal with an unpleasant person. You can make the unpleasant person a babysitter, a teacher, a nurse taking care of a sick person, a boss, or any other character you wish. Be sure to show your unpleasant person in action. Don't just tell about him or her.

Writer's Triangle © 1989

One More Flight

by Eve Bunting
(Frederick Warne, 1976
out of print;
available only in paperback,
Dell/Yearling, 1979,
ISBN 0-440-46640-7).
Realistic Fiction.

Summary: When 11-year-old Dobby runs away from the Residential Treatment Center for the ninth time, he meets Timmer, an older boy who cares for injured birds of prey in an old barn. Dobby is fascinated by Timmer and the rehabilitation center he has established. Realizing that Timmer is also without a family, he fantasizes living with him and helping with the birds. Timmer helps him see that this is not possible. Using a real, analogous situation with the birds, he shows him that freedom is something for which one must be ready. At the end, when Dobby is about to return to the home, we know that he understands and accepts his present limitations.

Comments: *One More Flight* is a short, simple story, written in easy-to-read and -understand language. Nevertheless, it deals with a serious subject and raises interesting discussion questions. It is therefore a good book to use with less sophisticated readers.

Prereading Focus

One More Flight
by Eve Bunting

Meet with your discussion group before you begin reading and talk about how you think people your age feel when they run away.

As you read, think about
▌ how Bunting tries to make us care about Dobby
▌ what Bunting would have had to learn before she could write this book

Schedule

Fact Check Test _____

Discussion _____

First Draft Due _____

Final Draft Due _____

Notes

_____

_____

_____

_____

_____

Writer's Triangle © 1989

| Fact Check Test |

One More Flight

by Eve Bunting

1. What did Timmer live in?

_____

2. Timmer had many scars on his hands. What caused them?

_____

3. Why did Dobby try to run away from Timmer?

_____

4. Why did Timmer set out empty cans, pans, and bells on a rope?

_____

5. Name things the birds need in addition to meat to keep their crops and stomachs clean.

_____

6. Where did Timmer get most of the food for the birds?

_____

7. What pet did Miss Bee carry under her arm?

_____

8. What damage did Dobby do the second time he tried to run away from Timmer?

_____

9. What special piece of clothing do you need to handle a hawk or falcon?

_____

10. What was Mr. Jacobs, the intruder, trying to do to the birds?

_____

One More Flight
by Eve Bunting

1. What did Timmer live in?

   a barn

2. Timmer had many scars on his hands. What caused them?

   birds, or beaks, or talons of birds

3. Why did Dobby try to run away from Timmer?

   He was going to send him back to the home.

4. Why did Timmer set out empty cans, pans, and bells on a rope?

   to make an alarm system

5. Name things the birds need in addition to meat to keep their crops and stomachs clean.

   fur, bones, etc.

6. Where did Timmer get most of the food for the birds?

   animals killed on roads

7. What pet did Miss Bee carry under her arm?

   rooster

8. What damage did Dobby do the second time he tried to run away from Timmer?

   He smashed the fender of the jeep and knocked down the gas station sign.

9. What special piece of clothing do you need to handle a hawk or falcon?

   a long, heavy leather glove

10. What was Mr. Jacobs, the intruder, trying to do with the birds?

    set them free

One More Flight

by Eve Bunting

Note: Page numbers here are for the Dell/Yearling paperback edition.

SETTING

Why did Bunting set this story in an isolated area?

▌ The isolation of the area sets a mood for us, helps us feel Dobby's isolation from people.

▌ The wilderness is an appropriate setting for the birds of prey that play such a large part in the story.

▌ We can believe that, in a rural community such as this one, a boy from a home would be quickly identified and cared for. Timmer could get permission to keep him for a little while because the people who live in the area know and trust each other. In a city he'd just be picked up by the police and taken back to the home.

CHARACTERS

1. **Authors try to make us care about their characters. If readers don't feel interested in the characters and want to know what happens to them, they won't want to read the story. How does Bunting *try* to make us feel sorry for Dobby?**

   He's orphaned, lonely, often in trouble, scared in strange situations, and has daydreams that can't be fulfilled.

2. **For characters to be realistic, an author has to give them negative as well as positive qualities. Are there things about Dobby that you don't like?**

   Dobby lies, solves problems by running away, wants his own way, and acts without considering the effect. For example, he is so eager to get away that he starts the jeep without thinking about his lack of driving ability.

3. **Bunting makes Timmer the sort of teenager a boy like Dobby would really admire. What characteristics does Timmer have that attract Dobby?**

Timmer is independent and has a lot of freedom. He's different. He lives without parents and he doesn't conform to conventional ways of living. For example, he sleeps in a sleeping bag on the floor of the barn, he has an unusual job, and he eats informally—drinks from a jelly glass, puts dirty dishes on a shelf.

4. **How does Bunting make a minor character, Miss Bee, add interest to the story?**

Miss Bee is rich but she doesn't act as we would expect a wealthy person to behave. She dresses oddly in baggy pants and work boots even though she wears "about six big diamond rings on her fingers." Her hair is cut so short that it sticks up in little tufts all over her head. She wears a whistle on a string around her neck and carries a big white rooster.

5. **Mrs. Pruitt is someone we never see, but Bunting has her play an important role. Why do you think Bunting never has us meet her?**

Bunting wants us to see Mrs. Pruitt through Dobby's eyes. She is really a kind person, something we learn at the end of the book. If we knew it all along, we wouldn't care if Dobby went back or not. In order for us to sympathize with Dobby and remain interested in what happens to him, Bunting keeps us guessing about Mrs. Pruitt.

PLOT

1. **Every story has to have a conflict, a problem. It can be a battle with nature, with oneself, with society, or with another character. What is the conflict in this story?**

Dobby can't adjust to having to live in an institution. He has no choice, however, since he has no family and has a history of troubled behavior. This leads to conflict with the people at the home and elsewhere who try to help him. He doesn't trust them, and he resents them because he blames them for his being in the home.

2. **Bunting needs to show that Dobby changes over the course of the book, that he has grown in maturity and responsibility. How does she use the scene in which Dobby guards the birds from a suspicious stranger (pp. 90-99) to show Dobby's change?**

Writer's Triangle © 1989

Dobby is frightened and wants to run away, but he stays anyway. He also shows that he understands that freedom is not always a good thing. Dobby calls the stranger who tries to free them "stupid" and says that the birds would die because they were not ready to go.

3. Why does Bunting have Dobby get hurt when he defends the birds from the stranger?

It reinforces the bravery of his decision to stay and protect the birds. It emphasizes that doing the right thing can be difficult and painful.

LITERARY TECHNIQUE

1. Sometimes authors share ideas indirectly. They make action or characters symbols that stand for something else. They usually do this when they want their story to tell us a "truth."

A. What truth about freedom does Dobby need to discover in *One More Flight* and what symbol does Eve Bunting use to help him find it?

The truth is that we must be prepared for freedom before we can know how to use it. The symbol is the birds, which are sheltered, healed, and taught to cope before they are freed.

B. Why do you think Bunting uses birds as her symbol?

Birds are not tied to earth—they fly—so people have always seen them as a symbol of freedom.

C. Why does Bunting use birds of prey?

They represent strength and power, but even they can be free only when ready.

2. Another technique Bunting uses is to write some parts in italics. Which parts of the story are written in italics?

Dobby's thoughts when he is having a fantasy are italicized.

What effect does this use of italics have on the reader?

It lets us know Dobby better. It builds sympathy for him by revealing the difficulties he's experiencing in his life.

One More Flight
by Eve Bunting

CHOOSE ONE WRITING ACTIVITY THAT INTERESTS YOU.

A. How do you avoid making a story sound like an encyclopedia article when you have factual information to give your reader? One trick is not to tell everything in one paragraph or speech. People can talk to each other about the subject. One person can ask questions and the other give answers, or both can search for the information.

Choose a bird to research. It can be a bird of prey, a garden bird, or a water bird. Look up information about your bird. For the first part of your assignment write a list of interesting facts that you may want to include in a story.

For the second part of your assignment write a scene in which people are talking about the bird. Use dialogue to work in factual information in an interesting way. You don't have to use all your facts, but you should include enough so that the reader learns about your bird. To make the scene interesting, have some other things going on at the same time. Your characters can move around, touch things, react to each other, and if the bird is in your scene, they can react to the bird.

B. Suppose Dobby didn't find Timmer when he ran away. What might have happened to him? Create an adventure for Dobby in this new situation.

Writer's Triangle © 1989

The Sign of the Beaver

by Elizabeth George Speare
(Houghton Mifflin, 1983,
ISBN 0-395-33890-5;
in paperback,
Dell/Yearling, 1984,
ISBN 0-440-47900-2).
Historical Fiction.

Filmstrip set
(Cat. #676-31082-6),
VHS (Cat. #676-27795-0),
and **listening cassette**
(Cat. #676-31090-7) are
available from Random
House Media, Dept. 437,
400 Hahn Road,
Westminster, MD
21157-9939.

Summary: When Matt's father leaves him in charge of their newly built homesteading cabin in Maine in order to return to Massachusetts to get the rest of the family, Matt runs into some trouble. First a wanderer steals his rifle, then he is badly stung by a swarm of bees. Befriended by Indians, Matt agrees to teach Attean, a boy about his age, to read. In exchange Attean brings him food and teaches him to live in the woods. They do not start as friends, however, and much of the book is about Matt's effort to win Attean's respect. Matt learns to abandon his prejudices about Indians as he learns to take care of himself.

Comments: *The Sign of the Beaver* is a splendid survival story with an interesting, positive view of Indians and life in pioneering days. There is much room for discussion about prejudice, courage, and decision making (Matt must decide at the end whether to wait for his parents or travel west with the Indians).

Prereading Focus

The Sign of the Beaver
by Elizabeth Speare

Meet with your discussion group before you begin reading and talk about what it might have been like to be all alone waiting for your family and living in a wilderness cabin in the 1700s.

As you read, think about
- what Speare has Matt learn in order to survive in the wilderness
- how Matt's relationship with Attean and the other Indians changes over the course of the book and what events Speare has included that bring about this change

Schedule

Fact Check Test _____

Discussion _____

First Draft Due _____

Final Draft Due _____

Notes

_____

_____

_____

_____

_____

Name _____   Room _____

 Fact Check Test

The Sign of Beaver
by Elizabeth Speare

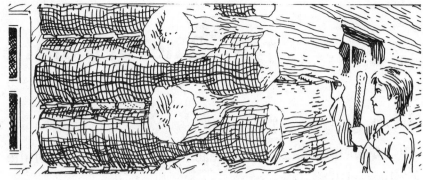

1. How did Matt's father teach him to keep track of the weeks?

_____

2. What did Attean's grandfather want Matt to teach Attean?

_____

3. What did Matt use to chink (fill up) the spaces between the cabin logs?

_____

4. What did Ben steal from Matt?

_____

5. What almost killed Matt at the beginning of the story?

_____

6. What did Attean use to catch fish?

_____

7. Why did Attean's grandmother hate white people?

_____

8. How did Attean's grandmother learn to respect Matt?

_____

9. What did Attean give Matt that helped him survive the snow?

_____

10. Why didn't Matt's family arrive in Maine on time?

_____

The Sign of the Beaver
by Elizabeth Speare

1. How did Matt's father teach him to keep track of the weeks?

   Matt should make seven notches on a stick.

2. What did Attean's grandfather want Matt to teach Attean?

   He wanted Matt to teach Attean how to read.

3. What did Matt use to chink (fill up) the spaces between the cabin logs?

   He used clay from the riverbank.

4. What did Ben steal from Matt?

   Ben stole the gun.

5. What almost killed Matt at the beginning of the story?

   Bees almost killed Matt.

6. What did Attean use to catch fish?

   He used wooden spears and wooden hooks.

7. Why did Attean's grandmother hate white people?

   They killed Attean's parents.

8. How did Attean's grandmother learn to respect Matt?

   Matt saved Attean's dog from the trap.

9. What did Attean give Matt that helped him survive in the snow?

   Attean gave Matt snowshoes.

10. Why didn't Matt's family arrive in Maine on time?

    They got sick with typhus.

Discussion Guide

The Sign of the Beaver
by Elizabeth Speare

Note: Page numbers are for the Dell/Yearling paperback edition.

PLOT

1. Was it right for Matt's father to leave him alone in the cabin? Why or why not?

Right: Children grew up early and were expected to be self-reliant. If a cabin were left unattended, it might have been taken by someone. Matt's father expected to be back soon.

Wrong: Matt was young and not sufficiently skilled as a woodsman. Dangers abounded in the wilderness: animals, Indians, bad weather, sickness, injury, people like Ben.

2. How does Speare's decision to have Matt's father leave Matt alone in their homestead affect the plot of the book?

It is the moving force of the book. Without it, nothing that follows would happen.

3. Why does Speare make the Indian boy, Attean, not like or respect Matt in the beginning of the book?

She helps us see Matt's development, or character growth. This device becomes an element of suspense that moves the book forward: will Matt be able to earn Attean's respect? Also, Matt starts to see himself through the Indian boy's eyes and reassesses himself.

4. Why did Speare make Matt's decision to stay in the cabin and wait for his family the point at which Attean really respects him?

It was a courageous decision. Most of the other things Matt learned to do, Attean could do better.

SETTING

1. How does the author use the book to teach us about life in this country at an earlier time?

Details of hunting, the cabin, and farming show us frontier problems. Details of Attean's hunting and life style as well as pictures of the Indian village give us comparisons. Matt's experience of living alone conveys the loneliness of frontier life and the dangers pioneers faced. We learn the importance of self-reliance, self-discipline, and adaptability.

2. How did the setting of Speare's story contribute to the suspense in the book?

Isolation in a wilderness meant that Matt couldn't get to other white people and had to rely on his own ingenuity and help from the Indians.

3. Why did Speare write a historical fiction novel instead of a history book?

It's more exciting this way. We get the point of view of the participants, and the book shows the feelings of characters. We see the complexity of history: Attean and Matt experienced "history" differently. Speare challenges us to evaluate alternatives in history: the white viewpoint versus the Indian viewpoint.

CHARACTER

1. Read pages 11 and 12. What clues does Speare give us that alert us to Ben's dishonest character?

▮ Ben's physical characteristics: fat bulging under a ragged army coat, small blue eyes that glitter.

▮ Ben's behavior: look to see if Matt's father is around and questions Matt about his father, pushes Matt into asking him to stay for supper.

▮ Matt's response: uneasy, feels curl of alarm, muscles tense, shows unwillingness to answer, and finds himself lying.

2. Attean sneers at some of the chores that Matt does, calling them squaw work. Matt ignores these taunts. By creating this situation, Speare shows us things about Matt. What does she show?

Speare shows us Matt's self-confidence, his perception of reality. She shows us that he sees he isn't completely reliant on Attean, who seems to know so much.

3. How does Matt's preparations for his family's arrival show his caring and sense of responsibility?

He does what his father told him to do—and then some. He weatherproofs the house, harvests crops, makes a cradle and dishes and a doll for his sister. He eats less to save more for them.

Meaning

1. How does Speare use the way Attean's dog feels about Matt to reflect Attean's relationship to Matt?

The dog distrusts Matt in the beginning just the way Attean does. When Matt helps the dog, the dog begins to trust him as do the Indians. At the end he stays with Matt and we know he will love Matt. At this point in the story Attean is also ready to accept Matt as his brother.

2. How does reading *Robinson Crusoe* to Attean show Matt that white people, or Europeans, tend to be smug and stupid in their relationship to Native Americans?

Attean is master in the woods. As Matt realizes this, he also realizes that *Robinson Crusoe* is a fantasy of a European. For example, Friday wouldn't have been his slave; Friday would have shown Crusoe how to live on the island.

The Sign of the Beaver
by Elizabeth Speare

CHOOSE ONE WRITING ACTIVITY THAT INTERESTS YOU.

A. Using nonfiction sources, read about life in an earlier time: ancient Egypt, Greece, or Rome; Europe in the Middle Ages; or the United States during the Civil War. Make a list of things from that era you might want to include in your scene. Then write a fictional scene in which a person your age who lives in that earlier time faces a dangerous situation.

   Although you are creating an imaginary scene (things that people say and do come from your imagination), be sure your scene is historically accurate (things people wear and use, major events, and places come from history).

B. Survival is a major theme in *The Sign of the Beaver.* Matt needs to learn how to make a bow and arrow, traps, warm clothing, and so on. Pick a period of history and look up one of the following: how to make a simple boat (such as a canoe), how to make a simple shelter (such as a sod house), or how to make a weapon from ancient time.

   Write a fictional scene in which a person your age must make or learns how to make one of the above objects. Be sure it is historically accurate (use techniques, setting, and dress from that period) even though you are creating an imaginary scene.

This Time of Darkness

**by H. M. Hoover
(Viking, 1980,
ISBN 0-670-50026-7;
in paperback,
Penguin/Puffin, 1985,
ISBN 0-14-031872-0).**
Fantasy/Science Fiction.

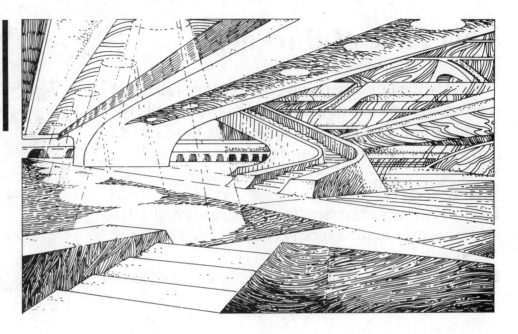

Summary: Amy lives in the future in an underground labyrinth of tunnels and corridors, the lower level of a domed city. Life is bleak and boring, and when the boy, Axel, claims to come from "outside," she believes him. Together they plan their escape back to his own people. It is not easy. Watchers watch and authorities threaten. Nevertheless, having heard that there is sunlight on Level 80, they climb to the top and discover the truth of their situation. The authorities fear them because they know too much, and so they are exiled. This sends them on further adventure through the badlands of "outside" until they happily end up with Axel's family.

Comments: Exciting, dramatic, and frightening, this book is a stimulating and creative exploration of what could be in store for Earth. Although the protagonists are young (11), the ideas and style are suitable for mature students as well.

Name _____ Room _____

This Time of Darkness
by H. M. Hoover

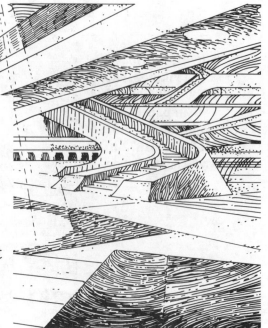

Meet with your discussion group before you begin reading and talk about what you think your daily life would be like if you lived in an underground society that was crowded, noisy, and dirty.

As you read, think about

▮ why Hoover's characters are able to accomplish what most people in their society couldn't even dream about

▮ what details contribute to the mood of horror Hoover creates

Schedule

Fact Check Test _____

Discussion _____

First Draft Due _____

Final Draft Due _____

Notes

_____

_____

_____

_____

_____

Writer's Triangle © 1989

Fact Check Test

This Time of Darkness
by H.M. Hoover

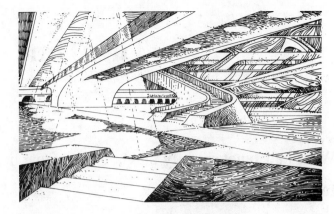

1. What had Janet secretly taught to Amy that helped the children escape?

   _____

2. Why didn't Valory want Axel or any other strangers in her house?

   _____

3. Before they got medical treatment in the decontamination area, the children had to do three things. Tell one.

   _____

4. At the last door leading to the domed city, Amy read a warning sign that helped her

   deactivate the _____ fire, which would have killed them.

5. Where did the old man in the domed city think people in his area got food?

   _____

6. What did Amy do to the "authority woman" who captured her?

   _____

7. What happened to Elton on the outside?

   _____

8. What happened to Amy's eyes on the outside?

   _____

9. What very human thing did James do right after he killed the wild men to protect the children?

   _____

10. What led Axel's father to the badlands, where he found the children?

   _____

This Time of Darkness
by H.M. Hoover

1. What had Janet secretly taught to Amy that helped the children escape?

   to read

2. Why didn't Valory want Axel or any other strangers in her house?

   She was jealous of her space. She was concerned about the cost of water and of waste. She didn't love Amy nor did she care if she had friends.

3. Before they got medical treatment in the decontamination area, the children had to do three things. Tell one.

   undergo vermin eradication; discard clothes; take a shower

4. At the last door leading to the domed city, Amy read a warning sign that helped her deactivate the _____ fire, which would have killed them.

   laser

5. Where did the old man in the domed city think people in his area got food?

   hydroponic farms under the city

6. What did Amy do to the "authority woman" who captured her?

   She bit her.

7. What happened to Elton on the outside?

   He was killed.

8. What happened to Amy's eyes on the outside?

   Her eyelids swelled shut, or she was almost blind from sunburn.

9. What very human thing did James do right after he killed the wild men to protect the children.

   He cried.

10. What led Axel's father to the badlands, where he found the children?

    Someone saw the fire, and the smoke came into the freight yard from the tunnel.

Writer's Triangle © 1989

| Discussion Guide | 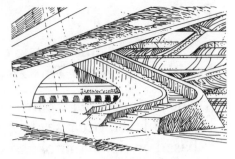 |

This Time of Darkness
by H.M. Hoover

Note: Page numbers here are for the Penguin/Puffin paperback edition.

SETTING

1. Authors of science fiction or fantasy have to make an imaginary world seem real. What details about the learning center and the halls does Hoover include in her first chapter to make her subterranean world come alive in our minds and horrify and frighten us? To help you, think about what Hoover makes us see, hear, smell, taste, or touch.

Details about the learning center include computer terminals and cameras and boredom (pp. 3-5). Scenes from the hallway include the screaming sirens and the need for earguards (p. 6), the hostility of passing people (p. 7), the use of ID cards (p. 7), the litter vac and loose garbage flying toward a suction screen (p. 7), the description of the roaches on the walls (p. 8), smells and contents of the fry shop (p. 8), the atmosphere in the supply depot (p. 9), the description of city-issue clothing (p. 9).

2. What do you think might have happened on earth to force people into domed, underground cities? Consider the clues Hoover gives us, both from half-remembered bits of history and from the children's experiences. Check pages 39, 75, 76, 119 for specific references.

Although a sudden disaster such as a nuclear explosion or reactor meltdown could have devastated the world, her clues suggest that human exploitation of the land and pollution of the atmosphere gradually reached a point where the earth became uninhabitable. One clue to this explanation is that the cities were tunneled out of solid rock, which would take time. The glass, plastic, and metallic shapes that protruded from the clay in the badlands suggest this, too (p. 101). When James describes how the cities developed, growing with no plan, like mold in the dark, and when he says waste buried them sometimes (p. 119), we know that the people haven't learned and are still polluting their environment.

PLOT

1. Every book has a basic conflict. Who are the children in conflict with throughout *This Time of Darkness*?

The basic conflict is between the children and the authorities. On a more subtle level, because the society is authoritarian and secretive and is based on rigid control and suppression of the masses, everyone on the lower levels is suspicious and paranoid. This creates a situation in which the children are in conflict with everyone, because anyone could turn out to be a watcher or informer.

2. Why are the children able to succeed in finding their dream when most others in their society are not able to see beyond their daily grind?

The children are intelligent and able to read. Axel, having known another life, possesses a sense of urgency about getting back to it. Amy, too, is given a glimpse of a better way through her association with Janet, and this helps her establish a goal. People who have goals try harder than people who are aimless, and as a result they accomplish more.

3. Why does Hoover postpone telling us that there is an upper class in this society living in comfort in surface domes? In what way does it make the plot interesting?

The unknown is frightening, and so as readers, we worry with the characters as they encounter strange corridors, doors, and people. We would not feel the same suspense if we knew what they were going to find on Level 80. Also, keeping a "surprise" until the middle of the book suddenly injects new questions and issues that stimulate reader interest.

4. How does James, the crazy, who watches and follows the children, make the plot more suspenseful? Think about the effect of his presence when they are in the lower levels, what we feel when they see him in the yellow-and-black-striped guard car, and what role he plays when they meet again outside.

James adds tension. His periodic appearances make us worry that he's a watcher or an authority in disguise. This is confirmed by the scene in which the guards are scolding him for failing to grab the two children, and we are newly horrified by the conditions in which these people live.

Writer's Triangle © 1989

When he emerges again in the outside, he is first a source of anxiety—we worry that he is after the children—but then he helps the children and provides information to them and the reader.

CHARACTER

1. Who do you think becomes a crazy in Hoover's underground/domed society? Do you think the crazies are really crazy?

Anyone who doesn't conform is treated as if they were crazy. This would include intelligent people, people who have learned things that don't agree with the computerized education given in the learning center, and people who rebel.

Some of the crazies are probably really out of touch, but many are probably like James, people we would find normal in our society but who don't fit into the rigid mold of Hoover's authorities.

2. Authors have to make their characters distinctive so that the reader can tell one from the other. Think about Amy and Axel. How are they different from each other? How are they alike?

Amy is very practical. She does what needs to be done, pushing aside unpleasant thoughts or situations such as her mother's rejection of her, the information that the authorities were considering killing them, or finding Elton dead. She tries to depend on herself rather than on others. Axel is more emotional. He shows his feelings and is bothered that Amy never shows that she is afraid. He is more willing to trust than Amy is, although both children demonstrate trustworthiness. Axel is more involved with other people. He shows more interest in Elton than Amy does and becomes very upset when Elton is killed.

Both children are highly intelligent, curious, and willing to take risks to achieve something worthwhile. They are both supportive of each other and of anyone they realize is a friend. We see this in their relationship with James.

3. In the adventures the children have while escaping, at first Amy takes a leadership role. What past experiences does Hoover give Amy that makes her leadership logical and necessary?

Amy has been raised in the underground city, so she knows how to function there. She can help Axel get earguards, and she knows how to protect them from the roaches and rats. It is Amy who has heard about Level 80 and provides them with protomush for their escape.

Writer's Triangle © 1989

4. **When the children get to the upper level and then outside, Axel takes over. He has been raised outside, so he recognizes the food they are given on the upper level, knows about the sun burning, finds berries and eggs for them to eat, and has the knowledge and experience to lead them to his home. Instead of being pleased with his new confidence, Amy becomes uneasy.**

   A. **Why does she become afraid when he stops being scared and no longer "shuts out" the world?**

   She's afraid he'll think she's nasty or stupid and that she'll lose him as a friend.

   B. **Is Amy's fear about Axel realistic? Do people become afraid when someone close to them changes?**

   Yes. Her fear is realistic. Sometimes, when one person grows or changes, they go in different directions, have new experiences, and make new friends. We know, however, that Axel won't reject her. Axel cares about her, depends on her, and knows her well. He isn't really changing. The real Axel has been there all along, hidden behind the "shut off" behavior he assumed in the underground city.

5. **Why did Hoover create such a strange relationship between Amy and her mother?**

   Valory doesn't care about Amy. She'd rather watch the vu-screen than talk to Amy. She doesn't care if Amy is happy or has friends. She doesn't care if Amy leaves; in fact, she'd rather like her to go and give her the space. This relationship contributes to the mood of horror in the book and has the effect of making the reader glad when Amy runs away.

MEANING

Now that you've read *This Time of Darkness* and thought about Hoover's concern for our environment, what do you think she wants us to learn by reading her book?

Answers will vary but may include that she wants us to take care of our world so that the future she imagined will never happen.

Writer's Triangle © 1989

This Time of Darkness
by H. M. Hoover

CHOOSE ONE WRITING ACTIVITY THAT INTERESTS YOU.

A. *This Time of Darkness* opens in a future time after something forced the people to live in subterranean and domed societies. Imagine a situation that would force people to escape the earth's surface. Create a scene that gives a clear account of what happened and why it occurred. The scene should include details that show disagreements or conflicts between characters about possible solutions to their crisis. Be sure to include emotions and feelings. Think about how you would feel if your world were in danger of destruction.

B. Hoover has created a very realistic imaginary setting. One reason she is successful is that she involves all our senses so that we can fully experience Axel and Amy's world. For example, think about the scenes in the noisy, crowded, stinking hallways, the cockroaches, the rats, the crazies. In addition to what the halls looked like, we knew how they sounded, smelled, and felt. These setting details enable Hoover to create a sense of horror in both her characters and in her readers.

For your writing assignment, choose a place. You may select any place you would like to write about: perhaps a subway, a room you know well, your favorite outdoor spot, or a place that has frightened you. Close your eyes and picture yourself there. What do you see? What do you hear, smell, taste? Touch something. How does it feel? What emotions are you feeling? A good writer makes these kinds of things come together to create a certain mood. Think about what mood you want to create. It can be joy, fear, anger, excitement, horror, sadness, boredom, tension. Then weave your details together to create an interesting setting that effectively portrays your mood.

Tuck Everlasting

by Natalie Babbitt
(Sunburst, 1975,
ISBN 0-374-37848-7;
in paperback,
Farrar, Straus and
Giroux, 1975,
ISBN 0-374-48009-5).
Fantasy.

Summary: When Winnie Foster runs off to the wood behind her house, she meets the Tucks, who have found a spring that has given them eternal life. They are not happy; the wheel of life turns, but they are no longer a part of it. They have to keep moving so that people won't catch on. They cannot have a normal family life, nor can they make friends. They beg her to keep their secret. If people learn of it, the world will never be the same. Winnie agrees once she understands the implications, but it is not so simple. While the Tucks were telling their story to Winnie, they were overheard by the man in the yellow suit. It is his plan to sell the water to "the right people." Mrs. Tuck kills him to prevent this disaster, and Winnie helps the family escape. Before he leaves, 17-year-old Jesse Tuck gives her a bottle of the water to drink when she is 17 and invites her to be his bride. In the end, Winnie pours the water on a toad, opting for a normal life.

Comments: *Tuck Everlasting* is a well-written, well-paced story with fine characters and an unusually interesting philosophical question at its core. (Do we want eternal life on earth?) The murder of the man in the yellow suit raises a serious ethical question. (Is murder ever right or necessary?) Most important, the concept itself stimulates the imagination of the reader.

Prereading Focus

Tuck Everlasting
by Natalie Babbitt

Meet with your discussion group before you begin reading and talk about what you think would happen in your life if you never got older and would never die.

As you read, think about

- why Natalie Babbitt has made the Tucks poor, ordinary people
- what Babbitt is trying to say about the idea of everlasting life on earth

Schedule

Fact Check Test _____

Discussion _____

First Draft Due _____

Final Draft Due _____

Notes

_____

_____

_____

_____

_____

Fact Check Test

Tuck Everlasting
by Natalie Babbitt

1. Why didn't people of the town of Treegap ever go into the wood?

   _____

2. When Winnie's grandmother heard Mae Tuck's music box, what did she think it was?

   _____

3. From what danger did Winnie rescue the toad?

   _____

4. What did the man in the yellow suit take from the Tucks?

   _____

5. How did the man in the yellow suit get the Fosters to sell him their wood?

   _____

6. Why did Jesse give Winnie the bottle of water?

   _____

7. What did Mae Tuck do to the man in the yellow suit?

   _____

8. How was Mae Tuck to be punished for killing the man in the yellow suit?

   _____

9. How did Winnie help Mae Tuck escape from jail?

   _____

10. How did the Tucks learn that Winnie decided to live a normal life instead of drinking the water and living forever?

   _____

Tuck Everlasting
by Natalie Babbitt

1. Why didn't people of the town of Treegap ever go into the wood?

   The cows had made a path around the wood, so there was no comfortable way *through* it. Also it belonged to the Fosters, and the Fosters and the wood were both a little forbidding.

2. When Winnie's grandmother heard Mae Tuck's music box, what did she think it was?

   elf music

3. From what danger did Winnie rescue the toad?

   a dog

4. What did the man in the yellow suit take from the Tucks?

   their horse

5. How did the man in the yellow suit get the Fosters to sell them their wood?

   He told them he knew where Winnie was and would trade that information for the wood.

6. Why did Jesse give Winnie the bottle of water?

   So she could drink it when she turned 17 and marry him.

7. What did Mae Tuck do to the man in the yellow suit?

   hit him in the back of the head with the shotgun

8. How was Mae Tuck to be punished for killing the man in the yellow suit?

   She was going to be hanged.

9. How did Winnie help Mae Tuck escape from jail?

   She took her place, so that the constable wouldn't realize she was gone before the Tucks had time to get out of town.

10. How did the Tucks learn that Winnie decided to live a normal life instead of drinking the water and living forever?

    They came back and saw her tombstone in the graveyard.

Discussion Guide

Tuck Everlasting
by Natalie Babbitt

Note: Page numbers here are for the Farrar, Straus and Giroux paperback edition.

PLOT

1. One of the problems Natalie Babbitt had to solve when she wrote *Tuck Everlasting* was to figure out a way to separate Winnie from her family so that she could meet the Tucks and have all her adventures. What problem did Babbitt set up in Winnie's home that made Winnie decide to run off?

Her family is overprotective and overattentive. Winnie believes that she needs to get away from the watchful eyes of her mother and grand-mother so that she can learn what she can do on her own ("... something interesting—something that's all mine" p. 15.).

2. What is Babbitt trying to show us when she has the Tucks become so upset when Winnie stumbles on their secret?

Their distress shows how serious the problem is. They are willing to take the risk of kidnapping her in order to impress on her the dangers of letting the world know about the spring.

3. How does Babbitt's inclusion of the man in the yellow suit make the plot more intense?

He is the villain of the book. Without the man in the yellow suit, the story would not have any real conflict. His relentless and selfish pursuit of the Tucks for their secret and his plan to sell the water only to people he thinks deserve it make us see how quickly the magic water would create enormous problems for everyone.

If Babbitt had made Winnie the only antagonist in the book, the threat would not be grave. Winnie is a good girl who wouldn't give the Tucks away. The big question, therefore, would be whether she would decide to drink the water when she turned 17. Either way, her decision would not be critical to all humanity.

4. Why does Babbitt include the toad in her story?

The first job of the toad is to lure Winnie out of the safety of her yard. While he is free to hop off to the wood Winnie feels as if she were in a cage. His freedom encourages her to pursue her plan to escape. The toad is also symbolic. He is a plain, dull creature. In this, he is not unlike the Tucks, who are also very plain and plodding. Thus, all the creatures Babbitt destines to live forever have nothing glamorous about them, and their special "gift" brings them no special joy.

5. Mae murders the man in the yellow suit. What clues do we have that Babbitt thinks Mae's action was justified?

Babbitt has made Mae a kindly and good person. She is loving toward Winnie and gentle with her own family. This makes us disposed to like her and forgive her. When Babbitt has us view her through Winnie's eyes, we see her as someone who needs to be protected. When we meet her years later in the epilogue, we see that she is still concerned about Winnie, which endears her to us even more.

As for her attack on the man in the yellow suit, he was threatening to upset the whole order of life on earth. If his threat had been one that would affect only the Tucks, then we might see her behavior as selfish. Babbitt, however, has her risk her own freedom in the interest of a higher good, which makes Mae something of a heroine.

CHARACTER

1. Why does Babbitt make the Tucks the kind of people they are: simple, uneducated, kindly, and "plain as salt"?

The Tucks have to be people who can blend into the countryside. If Babbitt had made the people who drank the magic water very rich or powerful, living more or less public lives, then everybody would soon realize what happened to them.

They have to be good people, or, like the man in the yellow suit, they would have exploited the water. Then it wouldn't be a story about gentle people forced to make difficult ethical decisions but would have been a different book altogether.

By making the Tucks simple and uneducated, Babbitt makes us very sympathetic to them. We are impressed with their gentle wisdom, and their understanding of the way the world and the people in it function.

2. How does Babbitt let us know that the man in the yellow suit is evil?

From the beginning his behavior is sneaky and suspicious. He comes to Winnie's house, tracking the Tucks. He hides and listens when the

Tucks tell Winnie their story. He takes their horse. He blackmails the Fosters into selling him their wood (with the spring in it). Finally, of course, he reveals his plan to exploit the Tucks and Winnie and sell the water.

3. What does Babbitt show us about the Tucks when she has them feel such a strong attraction to Winnie and show her so much love?

One thing, of course, is that it reinforces that they are good and loving people. Their interest in her, however, seems abnormally strong, and after a while we realize that they are all hungry for contact with a normal "growing" child. It shows how isolated they are and how they have been separated from the rest of humanity by their immortality.

4. After Winnie returns to her family, she is different. It is as though some part of her had slipped away (p. 107). How has she been changed by her encounter with the Tucks?

After having lived in a very protected environment, she has been exposed to "life." She has seen good and evil in action. She has had to make an important ethical decision regarding the Tucks and their secret. She has witnessed what would become a murder when the man in the yellow suit dies. She is worried about Mae, wants to help her, and in fact promises that everything will be all right. The part that has slipped away is her innocence. She is no longer a helpless child, dependent on her family for everything. In some ways, she is now more knowledgeable and sophisticated than they are.

SETTING

1. How does Babbitt alert us to the mystery and secretive nature of the wood?

She says there is something strange about it. It has a sleeping, otherworldly appearance that makes you want to speak in whispers. The cows go around it, and this makes the road go around the wood and keeps the people from going in (pp. 6-7).

2. How is it helpful to Babbitt to set the story in a small town in the last part of the nineteenth century?

In a time before everyone had a Social Security number and a driver's license, it was easier for people to disappear without being tracked down. In less crowded times, it is easier to believe that a spring giving eternal life could bubble away and not be found, for example, by troops of campers. Setting the story in an earlier time also gives Babbitt a chance to have an epilogue in which we find out what happened to Winnie.

THEME

One of the ideas that Babbitt explores in her book is in the natural order of the world; things move in a cycle. The seasons, the sun and planets, the water in the rivers and oceans—all are part of the wheel that turns and turns and never stops. Why has the Tucks' departure from this wheel caused them such unhappiness?

They are now different from other people. They can't raise normal families and have a natural growing child to love. Miles could not stay with his family; his daughter would be an old woman now, although he is still a young man. Jesse never had the chance to grow up and find a wife and start his own life. They don't fit with other people, who are afraid of them and possibly jealous. Mr. Tuck wants to age and die. He is tired of being an outsider and wandering around the world endlessly.

Tuck Everlasting

by Natalie Babbitt

CHOOSE ONE WRITING ACTIVITY THAT INTERESTS YOU.

A. There are a number of places in *Tuck Everlasting* where, had things gone differently, the story would have changed drastically. Choose one of these places and think of how things would have been if Natalie Babbitt had decided to go in another direction. Then write the changed scene as you picture it. Be sure to include your main character's feelings and details about the setting and other characters.

   1. Suppose instead of pouring the water on the toad, Winnie waited until she was 17 and drank the water Jesse gave her. Tell how she finds Jesse again, describe her meeting with him, and tell about their life together, both the good and the troublesome.

   2. Suppose the Tucks had not been able to get Mae out of jail. Write a scene in which the people of the town try to hang Mae. Give the details of the events of the day. Be sure to describe Winnie's feelings and tell how the other Tucks behave.

   3. Suppose Mae did not hit the man in the yellow suit. Can you think of another way to bring this story to a satisfying conclusion? Write an ending to the story that solves the problem without murdering the man in the yellow suit.

B. Natalie Babbitt begins her book with a prologue. This is a short introduction to the book in which we meet the critical characters and are told that they will come together in a strange way. She does not tell us the story's problem, but she does hint at something mysterious when she suggests that there are things better not tampered with in this world. Is there a book you are thinking about for which you could write a prologue? Try it. Make your prologue interesting, including hints of exciting or mysterious things to come, so that we will want to read your book.

The White Mountains

by John Christopher
(Macmillan, 1967,
ISBN 0-02-718360-2;
in paperback,
Collier Macmillan, 1970,
ISBN 0-02-042710-7).
Fantasy/Science Fiction.

Summary: Will lives in a future time when technology has reverted to a primitive state. No longer are there any cities, so people live in small, rural villages. The world has been taken over by Tripods, which take young people at age 14 and "cap" them so that they can be controlled. Will learns about a stronghold of freedom in the White Mountains from Ozymandias, a Vagrant who comes through his village. Will and his cousin Henry run off to find it, picking up Beanpole (Jean-Paul) as they pass through what is today called France. Here, Will is almost distracted from his quest when he is taken into a medieval castle and made one of the family. At the end of the book, they make it to Switzerland and the White Mountains.

Comments: This is a well-written and exciting adventure story. The theme is that freedom is crucial to happiness in intelligent people, and gaining it is worth considerable risk. Will decides that it is more important than a life of comfort and leaves a castle and wealth to pursue a life of hardship in which he can control his own mind.

Name _____ Room _____

Prereading Focus

The White Mountains
by John Christopher

Meet with your discussion group before you begin reading and talk about whether you would choose a life of luxury in which outside forces controlled your mind or a life of hardship in which you had freedom of thought.

As you read, think about

▪ how we know *The White Mountains* is science fiction and whether it takes place on our planet
▪ whether the conclusion of the book feels right to you
▪ how the poem "Ozymandias" is connected to the book (Christopher names one of the characters Ozymandias and quotes lines from the poem)

Ozymandias
I met a traveller from an antique land
Who said: Two vast and trunkless legs of stone
Stand in the desert. Near them, on the sand,
Half sunk, a shattered visage lies, whose frown,
And wrinkled lip, and sneer of cold command,
Tell that its sculptor well those passions read
Which yet survive, stamped on these lifeless things,
The hand that mocked them, and the heart that fed:
And on the pedestal these words appear:
"My name is Ozymandias, king of kings:
Look on my works, ye Mighty and despair!"
Nothing beside remains. Round the decay
Of that colossal wreck, boundless and bare
The lone and level sands stretch far away.
                                    —*Percy Bysshe Shelley*

Schedule

Fact Check Test _____

Discussion _____

First Draft Due_____

Final Draft Due_____

Name _____ Room _____

Fact Check Test

The White Mountains
by John Christopher

1. How did Jack and then Will get into the Tripod?

   _____

2. Who told Will about the stronghold in the White Mountains?

   _____

3. What happened to Will when he and Henry ran away from the sheep?

   _____

4. What powered the Shmand Fair carriages that moved on rails?

   _____

5. The boat carrying Captain Curtis and the boys almost sank. What caused the dangerous waves?

   _____

6. How did Beanpole first help Will and Henry?

   _____

7. What did Will take from the jewelry shop in the City of the Ancients?

   _____

8. What happened when the boys pulled the rings on the metal eggs they found in the City of the Ancients?

   _____

9. What did Will see when he pulled off Eloise's turban?

   _____

10. What operation did the boys have to perform on Will in order to escape from the pursuing Tripods?

    _____

The White Mountains

by John Christopher

1. How did Jack and then Will get into the tripod?

   A tentacle pulled them up.

2. Who told Will about the stronghold in the White Mountains?

   Vagrant, or Ozymandias, told him.

3. What happened to Will when he and Henry ran from the sheep?

   He sprained his ankle, or he hurt his leg.

4. What powered the Shmand Fair carriages that moved on rails?

   Horses powered the carriages.

5. The boat carrying Captain Curtis and the boys almost sank. What caused the dangerous waves?

   The Tripods caused the waves.

6. How did Beanpole first help Will and Henry?

   He helped them escape from the basement/dungeon/tavern.

7. What did Will take from the jewelry shop in the City of the Ancients?

   He took a watch.

8. What happened when the boys pulled the rings on the "metal eggs" they found in the City of the Ancients?

   The eggs exploded.

9. What did Will see when he pulled off Eloise's turban?

   Her head was bald, or he could see she was capped.

10. What operation did the boys have to perform on Will in order to escape from the pursuing Tripods?

    They cut a metal tracking device from under his arm.

Writer's Triangle © 1989

Discussion Guide

The White Mountains
by John Christopher

SETTING

1. How does the author give us clues that this story is science fiction?

He sets it in a future time and includes something unknown to us today: capping.

2. How does Christopher use the watch to give us clues to the time frame of the story?

By telling us the watch comes from an earlier time, we know the story takes place in the future in a less technological time.

3. Why does Christopher give us clues and not just tell us the time of the story?

He creates mystery this way.

4. Where does the story take place? How do you know?

After they respond, use an atlas to trace the boys' journey. The story takes place in England near Winchester, moves across the English Channel to Paris, and then on to Switzerland. We know where they are because Christopher gives hints about location: he names Winchester, mentions a water crossing and language change, tells about the City of the Ancients where there is a Metro, and identifies mountains to the south.

5. What are the White Mountains?

The Swiss Alps are the white, snow-covered mountains to the south.

MOOD

1. How does Christopher set a mood of suspense in the early chapters?

He only hints about what the strange thing capping might be. We know it's going to happen to Jack and we get clues that it's something to worry about. We know that Will is out of sync with his family and his community and we don't quite know why. Ozymandias says strange things.

2. Why does Christopher wait so long to tell us what capping is?

It adds mystery and suspense, making us curious.

CHARACTERS

1. What does Christopher show you about Will in Chapter One that prepares you for his running away?

Will's taking of the watch and going to the hide-out show his curiosity, his unwillingness to obey the rules, and his independence.

2. Why do you think Christopher presents Henry as a bully at first?

It creates tension and problems for Will, which allows us to see aspects of his character we might not otherwise see, and it gives Christopher a chance to show Jack being a good friend to Will.

3. What is Jack's role? Why did the author put him in at all?

The change in Jack shows what capping does. It helps to create urgency about capping and reveals Will's character.

4. How does Christopher make Ozymandias interesting?

He's a strange character. Although he seems to be crazy, we realize that in between the crazy words, he's asking Will sensible questions. We understand, as does Will, that Ozymandias may represent a clue to what's wrong with Will's society and may even offer a way for Will to escape.

CONFLICT

1. Every story has to have conflict, a problem. It can be a battle with nature, with oneself, or with another character.

Where is the conflict in this story?

The major conflict is between the Tripods and the people.

2. How does the author use the conflict with the Tripods to bring in suspense and fear?

Writer's Triangle © 1989

The Tripods are a controlling object, which is scary. We don't know what the Tripods are, and we are afraid of the unknown.

3. What do you guess the Tripods might be?

They might be alien beings or instruments of alien beings.

4. When Will is in the count's castle, he experiences a new kind of conflict. (This is called internal conflict.) Will wants two different things. What are the two things he wants?

Will wants to escape to the White Mountains, and he wants to live the "good life" in the castle with Eloise and her family.

5. Why does Christopher make the count's castle so enticing?

It shows Will's human weakness. We understand the depth of his commitment to freedom when we see how much he's willing to give up.

6. Throughout the book, Christopher has the closeness of the boys' friendship shift back and forth. Where does this happen?

Henry starts as an enemy and then becomes a partner and helps Will when he's hurt. Beanpole and Henry become close in the City of the Ancients, and Will feels left out. The trend continues in the castle when Will is cosseted by Eloise's family.

7. How do the boys' shifting alliances affect the story?

These shifting alliances provide more tension, interest, and excitement and expand the book. All the scenes in which the alliances shift would not be there without these conflicts.

MEANING

1. Why do you think Christopher chose the symbol of the White Mountains as a goal?

White often stands for goodness or purity. The mountains are taller than the Tripods, making them more powerful. A mountain is something to climb, making it a good symbol for a goal.

2. Why does Christopher have the Vagrant Ozymandias recite the poem that says, "Look on my works, ye mighty, and despair"?

It gives a clue that the name Ozymandias comes from a poem written in an earlier time. It suggests the impermanence of those with power and

Writer's Triangle © 1989

control, encouraging the boys to fight their present situation. It foreshadows the ruined city the boys travel through later in the book. The combination of madness and sanity is interesting.

3. What is Christopher really trying to say to his readers?

He wants to talk about the hunger for freedom and democracy and to explore individual rights versus responsibility to family and society.

4. Do you think Will's conflict is realistic? For example, do you think any of the people who left their homes in Europe or Asia to come to America faced similar decisions?

Yes, Puritans came for religious freedom; many others came to escape oppressive governments, like the refugees from Vietnam, the Soviet Union, and Iran.

CONCLUSION

1. What were your feelings about the conclusion of the story? Did Christopher do a good job with the ending?

Answers will vary.

2. What more might he have done for us?

He could have told more about the last part of their journey. It would have been interesting to hear how they got from the foothills to the fortress and have them congratulated for their successful escape. We might have liked to learn more about the Stronghold.

3. Why do you think Christopher didn't include these things?

Answers will vary. Possibly he was saving some things for his sequel.

The White Mountains

by John Christopher

CHOOSE ONE WRITING ACTIVITY THAT INTERESTS YOU.

A. In the opening chapter, Christopher gives us hints about the time his story takes place. Write an opening paragraph to a story that you set in another time or place—just give hints. We will share our openings and see if we can guess each other's settings.

B. Expand the conclusion of *The White Mountains* by writing a scene in which we learn how the boys got to the fortress from the foothills and how they are welcomed on their arrival. Think about the difficulties of climbing the Alps with Will being injured. Consider, too, how they would locate the well-hidden stronghold.

Words by Heart

by Ouida Sebestyen
(Little, Brown/Atlantic
Monthly Press, 1979,
ISBN 0-316-77931-8;
in paperback,
Bantam/Starfire, 1987,
ISBN 0-553-25900-8).
Historical Fiction.

Summary: It is 1910, and Lena Sills and her family have left Scattercreek, their comfortable southern black community, to try to better themselves out west in Bethel Springs. Possessed of a "magic mind," Lena wins a contest for reciting Bible verses. When the family gets home from the contest, they find a warning knife stabbed through a freshly baked loaf of bread. It is the work of the Haneys, jealous, angry sharecroppers on Mrs. Chism's land. Sebestyen spends a lot of the book building the tender, loving relationship between Lena and her father, showing how he guides her through some difficulties with Mrs. Chism and how he teaches her love and understanding for her enemies. After Lena's father dies from a gunshot wound inflicted by Tater Haney, Lena is torn between her anger and her father's lessons of love even for one's enemies. She has assimilated her father's goodness, however, and she accedes to his dying wish and brings the injured Tater home, saving his life. In a symbolic reconciliation, the last image of the book is of Mr. Haney picking the Sillses' cotton to help out.

Comments: A powerful book exploring risk and courage, hate and love, ignorance and understanding, *Words by Heart* offers a picture of the life of the black family and its struggles to maintain dignity in a hostile environment.

Prereading Focus

Words by Heart
by Ouida Sebestyen

Meet with your discussion group before you begin reading and talk about what you would do if you were really poor and there was no one outside your family to help you get ahead.

As you read, think about

▮ how the Sills family copes with the problems of being poor and black

▮ what things Lena learns over the course of the book that make her a better, more mature person

Schedule

Fact Check Test _____

Discussion _____

First Draft Due _____

Final Draft Due _____

Notes

_____

_____

_____

_____

_____

_____

Writer's Triangle © 1989

Fact Check Test

Words by Heart
by Ouida Sebestyen

1. What was the prize for the Bible verse recitation contest?

   _____

2. What happened to the bread that Lena's stepmother had left on the table to cool when they went to the contest?

   _____

3. What happened to Lena's dog, Bullet?

   _____

4. What did Lena take from Mrs. Chism's house?

   _____

5. Why couldn't Lena's papa find Mrs. Chism's wire and fence posts at the Haney's barn?

   _____

6. Who enjoyed memorizing verses and tried to be Lena's friend?

   _____

7. What happened to Sammy Haney's turnip lunch?

   _____

8. Who came to Mrs. Chism's party?

   _____

9. How was Tater injured?

   _____

10. How did Mr. Haney help Lena's family after her papa died?

    _____

Words by Heart

by Ouida Sebestyen

1. What was the prize for the Bible verse recitation contest?

   a blue bow tie

2. What happened to the bread that Lena's stepmother had left on the table to cool when they went to the contest?

   Someone stabbed a butcher knife through one of the loaves.

3. What happened to Lena's dog, Bullet?

   He died; possibly he was poisoned or hit.

4. What did Lena take from Mrs. Chism's house?

   books

5. Why couldn't Lena's papa find Mrs. Chism's wire and fence posts at the Haney's barn?

   The Haneys had sold them.

6. Who enjoyed memorizing verses and tried to be Lena's friend?

   Winslow

7. What happened to Sammy Haney's turnip lunch?

   The children threw it in the privy; or they threw it away.

8. Who came to Mrs. Chism's party?

   Mr. Jaybird Kelsey

9. How was Tater injured?

   His horse bolted and dragged him.

10. How did Mr. Haney help Lena's family after her papa died?

    He picked their cotton.

Writer's Triangle © 1989

Words by Heart
by Ouida Sebestyen

Note: Page numbers here are for the Bantam/Starfire paperback edition.

SETTING

Why do you think Sebestyen made this book with its racial tensions take place outside of the Deep South?

She wanted to show how Lena's family left the South to search for a place where they could leave racism behind and better themselves. She also wanted to show that racism is not confined to a single place or people. Removing the story from a stereotypic situation enables her to explore the complexity of the difficulties faced by poor black people. Their problems seem to be circular. Because they are black, they have trouble getting ahead, and because they are poor, they have problems becoming educated and finding good jobs.

CHARACTER

1. **Good authors show that a character learns things and changes over the course of a book. What's the most important thing Sebestyen has Lena learn in *Words by Heart*?**

   Lena learns from her father to behave in a loving way no matter what people deserve. She proves how much of her father's teaching she has absorbed when at the end of the book she protects Tater, the boy who murdered her father.

2. **Sebestyen makes Lena's papa the most admirable character in the book. We have no doubt that, in spite of constant poverty, his life was more meaningful than were the lives of many richer people. In what ways was Papa's life a success?**

   He set high standards for his family and showed them how to achieve those standards. Sebestyen has him work hard, live according to the good things he learned from his religion, and try to understand and deal kindly with all the people he meets. She also makes him a fine teacher, explaining to Lena the importance of setting high standards (pp. 22, 24-25). His whole life is a monument to the importance of love, fairness, education, and honesty (see p. 55).

3. **Mrs. Chism is a selfish woman. As we watch her, we realize that she is always concerned about herself. How does Sebestyen show this selfish aspect of her personality?**

Many incidents reveal her selfishness: her refusal to lend Lena her books (pp. 35-36), her focus on her own feelings rather than the needs of her bird (pp. 42-47), her persistence in pushing Lena's father to put her fence posts in, and her demand that Lena work for her even on a school day (p. 29). After Papa's death she voices her irritation that she has lost a good hand, which seems insensitive (p. 132).

PLOT

1. **When we compare the Haneys with Lena's family, we realize that although they are both very poor and dependent on Mrs. Chism, Lena's family copes with the difficulties of their lives much better than the Haney family does. In what ways does Sebestyen have the Sills (Lena's family) behave better than the Haneys?**

Lena's family works hard. The Haneys don't. When things don't go well, Lena's family tries harder. The Haneys give way to anger and hostile behavior. Lena's family is honest (her father insists that they offer to make restitution for Mrs. Chism's books), but the Haneys are not (they stole the fence posts).

2. **How does Sebestyen make Mrs. Chism partly responsible for what happened to Lena's papa?**

She lets Mr. Haney stay on her property after she has fired him, which enables Haney to see Ben make a success of his old job. By forcing Lena's papa to confront Mr. Haney over the fence posts, Mrs. Chism sets up a situation in which Mr. Haney will be humiliated in front of his family and in front of Lena and her papa. She pushes the Haneys to the wall by saying she will take their horse as payment for the missing fence posts.

3. **Lena's success at the Bible verse contest and her family's successes in pleasing Mrs. Chism create some problems for them. What do you think Sebestyen wants us to learn about life for poor blacks by including these incidents?**

Any time Lena's family does well, ignorant, unsuccessful families try to stop their progress. Although the Haneys are the most dramatic

Writer's Triangle © 1989

example, Mrs. Chism also tried to feel superior by making unfair demands and treating them rudely. Mr. Doans, too, shows his ignorance by insisting that the whites are a superior race. In contrast, the more educated people, such as Winslow Starnes, admire the Sillses' strengths and are supportive.

4. Why does Sebestyen include the scene in which the children throw Sammy Haney's turnip around and finally dump it in the privy?

It shows Lena's mixed feelings. It lets the reader feel sorry for the Haneys, which prepares us for not hating them too much at the end. It shows that Lena is not at the bottom of the heap—Winslow is her friend. Sammy's smashing Lena's lunch foreshadows the attack on Lena's father.

LITERARY DEVICES

Authors generally give their readers hints about things that are going to happen in their books. They do this because we wouldn't like an ending that was not a logical outcome of what had come before. It would seem unreal and tacked on. Characters behave in certain ways and set chains of events in motion. *Foreshadowing* is what we call clues that authors give us to alert us to these chains of events.

In *Words by Heart,* Sebestyen foreshadows Papa's death in many places. How do each of the following incidents foreshadow his death?

1. The knife in the bread (pp. 14, 15)

The knife thrust into the bread is a violent act, a warning about what could happen to them. Ultimately, Lena's father dies violently.

2. Bullet's death (p. 26)

Bullet is murdered as Lena's father is going to be.

3. References to the Haneys (pp. 2, 16-18, 57-62)

The Haneys are often referred to as hostile, angry, and threatening. This warns us that something bad will happen.

Words by Heart
by Ouida Sebestyen

CHOOSE ONE WRITING ACTIVITY THAT INTERESTS YOU.

A. One way Sebestyen shows us about poverty is by comparing the sparsity of Lena's home to the more elaborate home of Mrs. Chism. She also shows us how poor the Haneys are when she compares Sammy Haney's turnip lunch to the wonderful things Lena has packed in her lunch. The Sillses' honesty and industry is emphasized because it is set next to the Haneys' dishonesty and laziness.

Try out this technique of comparison to achieve emphasis in your own writing. Write a scene in which you describe someone, and emphasize what you are saying by comparing your character to one with the opposite characteristics. You can use beauty and ugliness, intelligence and stupidity, liveliness and dullness, health and sickness, meanness and kindness, or any other pair of characteristics that interest you.

B. What do you think is going to happen to Lena now? Pretend you are Sebestyen and want to write a sequel to *Words by Heart.* Imagine what life will be like for the family without Ben Sills to help them. Who will take over the leadership in the family? How will they make enough money to survive? Will any of the neighbors help? Will Lena find a way to pull herself out of the cycle of poverty? Write a summary of the things you would put into a sequel to *Words by Heart.*

Writer's Triangle © 1989

A Wrinkle in Time

by Madeleine L'Engle
(Farrar, Straus and
Giroux, 1962,
ISBN 0-374-38613-7;
in paperback,
Dell/Yearling, 1973,
ISBN 0-440-49805-8).
Science Fiction.

Filmstrip set
(Cat.#394-77159-1) and
istening cassette
(Cat. #394-77157-5) are
available from Random
House Media, Dept. 437,
400 Hahn Road,
Westminster, MD
21157-9939.

Summary: Meg Murry's scientist father has been missing for a long time when she and her brother, Charles Wallace, meet Mrs. Whatsit, Mrs. Who, and Mrs. Which. These strange beings help them and their friend Calvin find her father. They cross vast space via a shortcut called a tesseract, or a "wrinkle in time." They learn that their father has been fighting the Dark Thing and has been imprisoned on the distant planet of Camazotz by IT. When they try to rescue him, Charles Wallace is pulled in by IT. The power of Meg's love ultimately saves them both.

Comments: Sorting through this complex, difficult book is well worth the effort. The fantasy is fascinating; the plot is tense and fast moving. The children in the book are "gifted" and suffer at the hands of classmates because of it, which makes the story helpful for the very bright reader who may have had similar difficulties. For the less able readers who have trouble following the book, the listening cassette is helpful.

Name _____ Room _____

A Wrinkle in Time
by Madeleine L'Engle

Meet with your discussion group before you begin reading and talk about how you would feel if your father were missing and you had a chance to rescue him by going on a dangerous mission traveling through space and time.

As you read, think about

- ■ how L'Engle makes her book interesting by having kids your age encounter fantastic things
- ■ how L'Engle shows us the value of individuals and their differences

Schedule

Fact Check Test _____

Discussion _____

First Draft Due _____

Final Draft Due _____

Notes

_____

_____

_____

_____

Name _____ Room _____

Fact Check Test

A Wrinkle in Time
by Madeleine L'Engle

1. What did neighbors and people at school think had happened to Meg's father?

   _____

2. What is there about Calvin that makes him get along so well with the Murry family?

   _____

3. What secret work has Meg's father been doing?

   _____

4. How did Mrs. Whatsit's gift of the bell-shaped flowers help the children?

   _____

5. What kind of magic animal did Mrs. Whatsit turn into?

   _____

6. Underline all the words that describe Meg's personality.

        selfish   loving   patient   stubborn

7. Why was the little boy with the ball punished on Camazotz?

   _____

8. What power did Mrs. Who's glasses give Meg in the transparent column?

   _____

9. Tell one thing Aunt Beast did to help Meg get well.

   _____

10. What made Charles Wallace break away from IT's control?

   _____

A Wrinkle in Time

by Madeleine L'Engle

1. What did neighbors and people at school think had happened to Meg's father?

   He'd gone off and left them.

2. What is there about Calvin that makes him get along so well with the Murry family?

   He is smart/thinks like they do/communicates well.

3. What secret work had Meg's father been doing?

   He'd been studying tesseracts, or wrinkles in time.

4. How did Mrs. Whatsit's gift of the bell-shaped flowers help the children?

   It helped them breathe.

5. What kind of magic animal did Mrs. Whatsit turn into?

   She turned into a horse with a human head, or a flying horse.

6. Underline all the words that describe Meg's personality.

   selfish   loving   patient   stubborn

7. Why was the little boy with the ball punished on Camazotz?

   He wouldn't conform/play like everyone else.

8. What power did Mrs. Who's glasses give Meg in the transparent column?

   Meg could go inside the transparent column imprisoning her father.

9. Tell one thing Aunt Beast did to help Meg get well.

   Aunt Beast gave Meg food, love, clothes, warmed her up.

10. What made Charles Wallace break away from IT's control?

    Meg's love enabled him to escape.

Discussion Guide

A Wrinkle in Time
by Madeleine L'Engle

PLOT

1. Several upsetting things happen to Meg in the beginning of the story: her father is missing, people are sneering, and she is doing poorly in school. Why does L'Engle make Meg have so many problems?

L'Engle wants us to care about Meg. By making her an interesting girl with all these problems, L'Engle hopes we will eagerly read the book to find out how she works through her difficulties.

2. Why does L'Engle include tesseracts in her story?

She is writing science fiction and wants to include something "scientific" that will spark our interest and excite our imaginations. Time-space travel has always fascinated people, and with tessering, L'Engle invents a plausible-sounding way to transport her characters. Tessering also connects the children to their father.

3. What is the major problem the children must solve in this story?

Meg and Charles Wallace's father, who has been studying tesseracts, has disappeared. They want to find him and bring him home.

4. Writers of fantasy and science fiction often set up a struggle between the forces of good and the forces of evil. These ideas are hard to show in concrete form, however. What symbol does L'Engle use in *A Wrinkle in Time* to represent evil, and what does she use to represent good?

The Black Thing, or Dark Thing, represents evil, and love represents good.

5. Find some places in the story where the Black Thing is used and tell why it is effective.

- Mrs. Whatsit shows them the dark shadow on Uriel. It chills Meg with fear, and she begins to fall unconscious. The flower helps her breathe. The Dark Thing appears on Uriel first so the children won't be too scared when they see it on Earth. Perhaps it is also easier to understand somewhere else.

- Happy Medium shows the children Earth, and they can barely see it due to the Dark Thing. The sickness of the shadow darkens the beauty of the Earth. The Earth is so troubled because the shadow has been there for many years.

- The Dark is within Camazotz, too. For example, the man (Prime Coordinator) at the end of the enormous room on Camazotz seems to contain all the coldness and darkness they'd plunged through. Also, Meg feels icy horror when she leaves the column without the protection of Mrs. Who's glasses.

- Meg freezes going through the Dark; we get scared with her. We see its power, and we see the antidote is love (from Aunt Beast), which foreshadows the end of the book.

6. Love is also difficult to show. How does L'Engle show the power of love?

She pulls Charles Wallace back with love. It is the prime motivation for the kids' search for their father. Aunt Beast's and Mrs. Whatsit's gifts of love save Meg from the dark IT.

CHARACTERS

1. How does L'Engle let us know who the main character is?

The book is written from Meg's point of view; she's always where the action is and always has an important role to play.

2. Why does the author make Meg the only one of the travelers who can go back for Charles Wallace?

From a writer's point of view, the main character must be the hero or the book will fall flat. The plot also makes clear that Meg is the only one with the necessary emotional connection to Charles Wallace. No one else would have been able to break through the barrier surrounding him.

3. One of the most interesting characters L'Engle develops is not even

Writer's Triangle © 1989

a complete creature. The Brain is an imaginative character that could be created only in a science fiction book. How does L'Engle make this strange character so compelling and powerful?

She shows its absolute control over the people in Camazotz. The image of a pulsating, quivering brain in a strange domelike building that shines with an ominous light is a frightening one.

We like to think we are in control of our own minds. It is creepy to think a brain can take us over and make us speak and act for it. People of Camazotz are terrified because they are punished by a painful "reprocessing," and facing the unknown IT is even more fearsome.

L'Engle's creation is also effective because it is an organ without a body. We view people not only as intellects, but also as emotional, feeling creatures. The Brain is an uncaring intellect with total power, but no feeling.

4. **One of the things L'Engle seems to be saying throughout the book is that we need to accept and value individual differences.**

   A. Why does L'Engle make Charles Wallace, Meg, and Calvin people who do not quite fit in?

Sometimes wonderful people—people who are creative and sensitive—aren't like everybody else. Only people who see things differently can see possibilities for change. Everyone is unique in something and has important things to contribute.

   B. Why do you think the author makes Calvin fit into the Murry family better than his own?

If we don't fit in one place, we may fit in another. L'Engle's decision to have Calvin fit into the Murry family connects him to Meg and shows us that Meg can be important to someone other than her own family.

   C. Why does L'Engle make Aunt Beast look the way she does?

Once again, L'Engle is showing that difference is not necessarily negative. Aunt Beast's appearance also brings in the "amazing" to capture our interest.

5. **Why does L'Engle need to include the magical characters, Mrs. Whasit, Mrs. Who, and Mrs. Which?**

L'Engle needs to have a way to move the children around in space and give them assistance in their quest.

SETTING

1. How do L'Engle and other science fiction writers capture our interest through their choice of setting?

Travel to strange places is exciting. The idea of a two-dimensional planet or a place where everyone must perform exactly the same way intrigues us and involves our imagination in the story.

2. Sometimes we can solve our problems more easily if we look at them in a new way.

A. Which of Earth's problems is L'Engle addressing when she shows us the society of Camazotz?

She is addressing problems of countries whose governments don't value individual ideas and differences, governments that are controlling and authoritarian and that operate by using control and fear.

B. Why do you think L'Engle decided not to use a real government here on earth to make her point?

Inventing Camazotz enables her to talk about a subject without people already having firm ideas about it, and gives her a chance to more easily show an extreme "what if" situation.

A Wrinkle in Time
by Madeleine L'Engle

CHOOSE ONE WRITING ACTIVITY THAT INTERESTS YOU.

A. A message L'Engle seems to want us to understand from *A Wrinkle in Time* is that everyone of us is a unique individual and that we must value our differences. Write a one-page description of yourself telling what makes you unique—how you are different from your friends.

B. Sometimes a TV show has minor characters who become so popular that the TV producers decide to give them their own show. Aunt Beast is an interesting minor character in *A Wrinkle in Time*. We know what she looks like and how she behaves. Use your imagination to create an entirely new story in which Aunt Beast stars, but keep all her characteristics described in *A Wrinkle in Time*.